WOMEN *of* GRANITE

WOMEN *of* GRANITE

THE HIDDEN LIVES OF NEW HAMPSHIRE WOMEN AS SEEN IN THE CEMETERY, 1674-1992

GLENN A. KNOBLOCK

AMERICA
THROUGH TIME®
ADDING COLOR TO AMERICAN HISTORY

For my mother, Ceceilia Ann (Delaney) Knoblock: a woman with an adventurous and creative spirit who passed those same attributes on to her son. Thank you!

America Through Time is an imprint of Fonthill Media LLC
www.through-time.com
office@through-time.com

Published by Arcadia Publishing by arrangement with Fonthill Media LLC
For all general information, please contact Arcadia Publishing:
Telephone: 843-853-2070
Fax: 843-853-0044
E-mail: sales@arcadiapublishing.com
For customer service and orders:
Toll-Free 1-888-313-2665

www.arcadiapublishing.com

First published 2021

ISBN 978-1-63499-351-7

Typeset in 10pt on 13pt Sabon
Printed and bound in England

ACKNOWLEDGMENTS

Throughout the course of researching and writing this book, I have had some help along the way. Indeed, it is true that no historian works alone; some of my work has been helped by the facts uncovered by earlier generations of New Hampshire historians (as the source bibliography at the end of the book demonstrates), but I have also been fortunate to gain help from my fellow New Hampshire historians of today. Because of the small size of New Hampshire, many of us know each other and collaboration and information sharing is usually a pleasant experience. That was certainly the case with the following individuals: Dr. Marcia Schmidt Blaine, Professor of History at Plymouth State University, for her support and encouragement and for providing copies of her research about our state's female tavern owners. Like myself, she has had a long association with the New Hampshire Humanities, and does great work in furthering the cause of our state history; historian and blogger Janice Brown, whose Cow Hampshire history blogs have long been a favorite of mine. She was particularly helpful with providing assistance as to the final resting place for WWI Army nurse Ruth Ferris Corey and for arranging for her family monument to be photographed by John Wilby. My thanks also to John Wilby for photographing Corey's monument at nearly a moment's notice and for kindly allowing the use of his photograph herein.

Thanks also go to Lisa and Dan Rothman of the New Boston Historical Society. I have known them for a long time now, and they have always been helpful in providing information and, needless to say, are both excellent researchers. Dan was very helpful in providing insights into Sevilla Jones and the Plantin family, while Lisa was likewise helpful and went above and beyond, not only providing information about Samantha Plantin and her family, but also in locating the portrait of her which is reproduced here with the society's permission. This is a hidden treasure brought into the light of day, which adds to our ever-increasing knowledge of the early African-American families who lived in New Hampshire.

I would also like to thank historian Valerie Cunningham of Portsmouth, with whom I have had the joy to work with in the past, for her assistance regarding Elizabeth Ann Virgil, and Peggy Johnson at the Cook Memorial Library in Tamworth for providing information about Lucy Blake as well as her photo.

In regards to photographs, thanks go to the following: Beth Knoblock and her mother, Eileen Widner, for taking the photographs found herein for the old churchyard in Hollis; Emiline Dehn-Reynolds, Library Manager, and Rebecca Chasse, photographic technician, at the Milne Special Collections and Archives at the University of New Hampshire for their kind and enthusiastic support in providing an image of the painting of Elizabeth Ann Virgil; Valerie Cunningham and the African American Resource Center in Portsmouth for the photo of Esther Mullineaux; and Alan Rumrill, Director of the Historical Society of Cheshire County for allowing use of the photographs of Catherine Fiske and Hannah Davis. Unless otherwise noted, all other photographs are by the author.

In addition to those listed above, it seems only appropriate to also note those women who have been a source of inspiration, support, and encouragement to me over the years. Of course, I could not have accomplished the completion of this book, or any of my others over the years for that matter, without the love and support from my wife, Terry (Hensing) Knoblock. She not only accompanied me on every journey across the state to find the women's gravestones herein discussed, but she has been my best friend and supporter for over forty years now. Then there is my daughter, Anna Knoblock, who, while she was unable to accompany me to these sites, was with me in spirit, and always is in everything I do.

I would also like to recognize the following women who have influenced me in ways big and small over the years: my sisters, Debbie (Knoblock) Minnick and Lisa (Knoblock) Ishee; my grandmother, Marion (Hunt) Knoblock; my great-aunt, Gertrude (Knoblock) Danby; sisters-in law, Patty (Hensing) Wemmer, Karen (Hensing) Murray, and Susan (Hensing) Butters; my mother-in-law, Norma (McCoy) Hensing; my nieces, Emily Wemmer, Gelsey (Minnick) Hood, Amy (Butters) Meyers, Kristen (Butters) Eckhardt, Katie (Murray) Johnson, Lizzie Murray, Betsy Knoblock, and Jennifer Knoblock; my daughter-in-law, Elizabeth (Widner) Knoblock; my niece-in-law, Pamela (Robertson) Butters; friends, Susan Reynolds, Cathy (Brown) Adoh, Linda (Brown) Young, Mildred Davis, Mary Mae Donan, Moyna Richardson, Cathy Plante, Sarah Veld, Jennifer Boyle, Shea Thompson, Brandy (Teets) Perillo, Karen Moore, Kerri Serven, and Delina Bickford.

Glenn A. Knoblock
March 2021, Women's History Month
Wolfeboro Falls, New Hampshire

CONTENTS

Introduction

For most of New Hampshire's history, as elsewhere in the United States, the state has been a male-dominated society, the voice of women from the past often overshadowed, over-looked, or ignored altogether. In some cases, their stories, their history—"herstory" if you will—has been recovered through extensive research, sometimes in legal documents, town records, or personal records and correspondence. However, the story of women in New Hampshire history can also be told, at least in part, from another source that is readily available: our historic burial grounds and cemeteries.

Indeed, the silent gravestones and monuments within their confines which mark the final resting places of women young and old can sometimes speak volumes, and by examining them, we can learn much about their place in society and how it evolved from early colonial times down through the end of the Victorian era, a period of over 200 years. These details carved in stone sometimes reveal to us the kind of day-to-day lives they led, as well as their accomplishments and the hardships and tragedies they endured, and by learning to "read" these gravestones, both literally and figuratively, and understanding their symbolism, these details help to bring back to life lives that have, for the most part, been long forgotten.

However, this is not just a book about cemeteries and gravestone art; it also offers up the stories of many women of the past. For some of these women, their stories are hidden in plain sight, if only we care to take a walk through the cemetery to find them, while in others, only a portion of that story remains, leaving it to the modern-day viewer to discover the rest of the story. In yet other instances, only a few clues into the life of a given individual are available, and the remainder is left unknowable. Whatever the case may be, the lives of many strong, accomplished, and interesting women of granite are out there waiting to be told, and that is what this book does, bringing their accomplishments and life details to a wider audience through a unique historical perspective. The women, and their gravestones, discussed herein offers a wide range of stories and experiences. For some of these women, the reader may already have an acquaintance, but most will, I suspect, be women you have never heard about until now. Some of them led incredible lives, while many, perhaps most, lived ordinary lives.

The details of these lives are of exceeding interest, some highlighting ways of life that are incomprehensible to us in the modern age, while others are timeless and eminently relatable. Either way, some interesting stories about the granite women of New Hampshire, and the gravestones that mark their final resting places, await your discovery.

Finally, the gravestones and monuments for the women discussed herein come from the cemeteries located in over sixty towns and cities located throughout the entire state. Some of the cemeteries in these locales, such as the Congregational Church Yard (Hollis) Point of Graves Cemetery (Portsmouth), and Blossom Hill Cemetery (Concord) are well-known sites where large and/or interesting collections of grave markers may be found, while many others are located in smaller towns in lesser-known cemeteries that are not commonly considered travel destinations. The fact of the matter is that in every community in the state, there are stories of granite women waiting to be told. What you may encounter in your future travels is unknown, but I know that there are countless stories out there waiting to be told and I hope this book sets you, dear reader, on the beginning of new and exciting travels.

Part I

Gravestone Traditions

1

SYMBOLISM AND FORM

One of the most fascinating aspects of exploring local cemeteries or burial grounds are the symbols often found on the gravestones and monuments within. An overview of these symbols, the meanings behind them, why they were used, and how they evolved over the years, provides a useful backdrop for this study, as does a review of the general burial practices followed in New Hampshire. In many cases, these practices would seem to have varied but little between men and women, but this is not always the case. Indeed, gender-based biases and traditions are almost always present in burial places dating from colonial times down to the twentieth century (where our study ends), if one knows where to look for them.

New England's early settlers first followed the customs they brought with them from old England. Following the death of an individual, burial would take place within a matter of days, usually within a town burying ground (often located adjacent to a meetinghouse), or a private burial ground located on family land. While in the old country, churchyard burials were the most common, in early New England, many burials took place on family land because towns were large in geographic size and family farms and homesteads were spread out, with some located miles from the public burial ground. In a day and age when the dead were carried from their home to their final resting place on the shoulders of family and friends, the concept of the private burial ground quickly became an accepted option. It is also important to understand that in early New England, and even up to the time of the American Revolution, burial grounds were not considered sacred spaces, but merely a utilitarian space to lay the deceased to rest, conforming to the then-prevailing Puritan-Congregationalist religious doctrine, which specified that the soul departed from the body at the time of death, and what was left was simply, as was marked on many a gravestone, "mortal remains."

Funeral rites in early colonial times were in general brief and subdued for the general population, though the wealthier or more prominent the deceased usually resulted in more elaborate social preparations, including the distribution of a type of jewelry known as "mourning" rings (keepsakes that were seldom worn, which often included an engraved skull or other images associated with death) and gloves to friends and associates of the deceased, while the processions to the final burial place were larger and final graveside rites more elaborate, sometimes involving multiple eulogies. Though death has often been said to be the great equalizer, it is often the case that wealth and social standing was, and still is, very visible within New England burial grounds, both in terms of immediate burial services, as well as later on when gravestones or monuments were erected.

New England society during colonial times, and for many decades after, was a male-dominated one, and when it came to the selection of a gravestone and the choice of wording on that gravestone, we can spot these gender differences, even if they are subtle at times, if we know what to look for. For the gravestones themselves, later called monuments, there are two distinct aspects to examine, the first being their strictly visual aspects, including the symbols carved upon them, but also their overall size and shape. The second aspect of these gravestones is the wording itself employed in their inscriptions and epitaphs, which can sometimes serve, in combination with the symbols, to give us a more complete "reading" of the life of the deceased.

The time which elapsed from burial to the placing of a gravestone or monument for the deceased in colonial times was widely varied and there was no normal convention on when, or even if, a gravestone should be erected. Many factors went into this decision, the first, and most important, of these being the economic status of the deceased and their family. Early on, such purchases were a major undertaking in many cases, as New Hampshire had no professional gravestone carvers residing here until the 1740s.

Prior to this time, gravestones were "imported," largely from Massachusetts, in such towns where carvers were established as Boston, Charlestown, Dorchester, and further north in Haverhill and Bradford, though some also came from as far away as Rhode Island and Connecticut. Orders placed for gravestones might require several voyages by land or sea, one to place an order and a later one to pick up the finished gravestone and bring it back to the local cemetery. In general, those families that were well-off financially could afford to purchase such "imported" gravestones. These first consisted of two components, the headstone and the footstone, placed at the head and foot of the burial site to mark its boundaries, later, beginning in about the 1830s, consisting of a single monument or memorial, the footstone no longer in use. In contrast, those of lesser means did not always have the financial ability to purchase a marker, and therefore their gravesites were either crudely marked with simple fieldstones upon which was carved but little information, while others were left unmarked altogether, or marked with natural objects. This might consist of a simple boulder or piece of fieldstone which was dug up nearby, or a simple wooden post, which, after less than five or ten years exposed to the harsh New England weather, would decay and eventually disappear altogether. It is likely for this very reason, at least in part, that the specific graves for New Hampshire's earliest residents, who first settled here permanently in the 1620s, are largely unmarked and the earliest professionally carved gravestones extant today are those from the 1670s.

It is also important to remember two other aspects of these early settlements, the first being that they were small in population and most everyone knew each other, if not by personal association, then through some other family, church, or business connection. Thus, when the deceased was buried in the town burying ground (sometimes referred to as "the yard"), everyone knew whose burial site was where. Secondly, we must remember that at this time in New England society, when they were still trying to carve a community out of the wilderness, life was about the here and now, combined with worry about the destination of one's soul after death. Most families were not worried, at least very early on, about posterity or preserving in stone their loved one's memory or achievements. These more worldly ideals would come about only decades later once a town was well-established. These conditions also held true in many of New Hampshire's rural towns that were settled late in the eighteenth century, where simple, home-carved gravestones were often used because of either convenience (there being no nearby professional stone carver), or cost issues. The stone found in Hampton for six-year-old Sarah Fogg, who died in 1701, was possibly erected due to matters of cost, as professionally carved gravestones were readily available near to this southern coastal town, while that for a woman, possibly a member of the Wedgewood family, known only as "Mrs. W," dated 1791, in Effingham was likely due to the fact that in this remote eastern town, there were no gravestone carvers practicing anywhere close by.

Given these early and rural traditions, it is not surprising that the oldest professional grave-marker found in New Hampshire today dates from 1674, some fifty years after the colony was established. This table-stone marker (now broken) is for a woman of high society, Hannah Cutt, who is buried in Portsmouth in Proprietors Burial Ground. She was the daughter of Dr. Comfort Starr of Boston (a founder of Harvard University) and

Sarah Fog(g), 1701, Pine Grove Cemetery, Hampton.

Mrs. W., 1791, Baptist Church Cemetery, Center Effingham.

the wife of John Cutt, who would later become the first president of the Royal Province of New Hampshire. While early gravestones were often procured for families of means, from the end of the seventeenth century onward, even women from working-class families would have professionally carved gravestones to mark their final resting places. However, these stones were typically smaller in size and cost correspondingly less. One excellent early example is the diminutive gravestone for Eleanor Messer "Loid" (Lloyd) dated 1697 and found in Portsmouth's Point of Graves Cemetery. She was the daughter of Gertrude Messer, a midwife, and carpenter Francis Messer, and married Portsmouth mariner Allen Lloyd by 1691, when their first child was born. Her stone was acquired by her husband during a trading voyage to Boston, it being carved by a well-known early gravestone carver there named William Mumford.

Despite the above examples, for those women who were from poor families, or those who outlived their husbands and lived for some years as widows (whether of the middle-class or poor), it was often the case that, upon their deaths, no gravestone would be erected to mark their final resting places. This was likely due to a variety of reasons, which include (but are not limited to) poor financial status and the lack of close family to see that a gravestone was erected. While these situations also applied to men who died in like circumstances, it was more often the case in general that a woman's grave would go unmarked among those families with a history of purchasing gravestones. Unfortunately, due to the fact that many early gravestones in New Hampshire cemeteries have gone missing over the years, detailed research in this area cannot always tell the full story. One example that illustrates these differences is the Evans family in Dover.

Hannah Cutt, 1674, Proprietor's Burial Ground, within South Street Cemetery complex, Portsmouth.

Elenor Loid, 1697, Point of Graves Cemetery, Portsmouth.

Robert Evans of that town died in 1697, leaving behind his wife, Ann Thompson Evans, as well as two sons, Joseph and Robert. Ann Evans supported her family, at least for a time, as a tavern-keeper in 1719, licensed, according to historian Marcia Blaine, "to keepe a publick house of Entertainment for the Town of Dover for Retailing of Strong Drinck and Entertainment of Stranggers and travelers." After her death in 1727, she was buried in the town's main burying ground, Pine Hill Cemetery, as was her son, Joseph, upon his death in 1751. While records tell us that there once an Evans gravestone here of some kind, we have no surviving details that tell us whether this was a family marker that denoted Ann's final resting place, as well as that of her husband, or whether this marker was for her son only.

When there is, however, a grave marker present, this presents an opportunity to learn more about the status of women in society, and the first aspect of these markers that strikes one is the visual symbolism that has been used. The making of gravestones was performed by a stonecutter, also called a gravestone carver or sculptor (and sometimes all three at varying times in their career). This trade was entirely a man's business, as were all of the heavy trades for much of New Hampshire's history, such as that of the blacksmith, cordwainer, or wheelwright, while women were employed in such trades as that of a dressmaker or milliner. The motifs these men carved into the gravestones they fashioned were dictated by traditions within the stonecutter's trade, augmented by their own individual artistic touches and influences. Examples of the factors that worked upon the stonecutter include the Bible and the images its passages created in their own minds, but also the sermons preached each week on the Sabbath, especially in colonial times, when church attendance was an all-day affair and hellfire and brimstone sermons by Congregationalist ministers was often the norm. Not everyone in colonial times could read the Bible, but they did understand the images that were very visible in the public cemetery.

Other influences include the work of stonecutters who had preceded them, their work easily found in the local burying ground, and learned, in some cases, while working as an apprentice in the shop of an established stonecutter, as well as those of such allied artistic trades as the cabinet or furniture-maker, or even those who painted decorative household murals. Of course, like any artist, gravestone carvers also had personal influences which we can only speculate upon—certainly their own beliefs and thoughts about religion in general, and likely the afterlife in particular, informed their carvings, but likely so too were they influenced by family and friends. While most every gravestone carver developed his own style, with a certain standardization found in his work, there are also those stones carved by many that are outside their standard designs, in some cases stunning works of art. How these one-of-a kind examples came to be created is uncertain. Likely influences include special orders from the family of the deceased, who had in mind a special design for their loved one, as is the case with many monuments even today. However, it is also likely that in some cases carvers were given direction by their client to create something special, the details left to their own imagination. We can then imagine the carver drafting a design on paper before putting chisel to stone, perhaps asking for input from his own wife or even a close friend of the deceased, maybe even the town minister. How many of the death's head, soul effigies, floral, and other decorative elements that are found on gravestones from colonial times down through the Victorian era were the result of feminine influence is, of course, unknowable, but it is not unreasonable to speculate that such influences were present.

The first and oldest motif, prevalent from early colonial times through the 1730s, was the winged skull, or death's head. This was a motif brought here by early New England settlers and thus was a familiar one to early settlers. While these winged skulls are found in a wide-range of artistic styles, each of them represents a duality of thought—the skull signifying in graphic depiction the mortality of everyone in society, young and old, rich or poor, man or woman, a picture in stone of how we will all eventually come to be. However, the wings attached to the skull signified the possibility of attaining heaven and the transformation from a mortal to a heavenly being. In the religious orthodoxy of the day, no early devout worshipper in New Hampshire could know for certain whether they might go to heaven or hell after death as the destination of one's soul was believed to be pre-ordained, and, at least early on, it was also believed that the good deeds one practiced throughout his or her life could not change that destination. So, all one could do was hope, this message made abundantly clear on the stone-carvings found in the public burial ground.

Of course, other decorative elements were added to the gravestones, either in the main carving area at top (the tympanum), surrounding the death's head, but also in the richly carved side borders. Here we often see accompanying images that remind us of our mortality, such as the pick-axe and shovel (the tools of the grave digger), as well an hourglass, sometimes winged, sometimes not, but always suggestive of the fact that everyone's time on this earth is constantly running to the end. However, there are more pleasing elements that are also found, including floral and fruit motifs, perhaps suggestive of the rewards of heaven, or pinwheel and swirling designs, which may be representations of the heavens. It should be noted that these oft-times stark portrayals of death were employed on the gravestones for individuals of all, without regard to gender or age.

For us today viewing these gravestones for a young woman like Mary (Moulton) Batchelder (died 1716) of Hampton, these images seem morbid and shocking to our senses. Her stone is interesting not only for its grinning skull, which features deep-set eye sockets above which are carved curly eyebrows, but also for the side borders which feature finely carved gourds. When viewed in the context of the religious beliefs for the time, they are much more understandable. Because this motif was in use before most of New Hampshire was settled, death's head-themed stones are found primarily in Seacoast area towns and those in the southern tier of the state closest to Massachusetts, where the gravestone carver's trade got its start in New England. Death's heads become less prevalent the further north one travels, and, once past Concord, almost no examples of them are to be found, as by the time these towns were settled during the French and Indian War of the 1750s and later, the motif was already outdated and out of fashion.

However, in the previously mentioned areas, the death's head does occasionally make a reappearance decades after the Great Awakening, usually in conjunction with either a deep personal tragedy or, on a more-broad basis, in times of great uncertainty and social upheaval, such as the time of the American Revolution from 1775–1784. While these later-day death's heads were rather simple in design and not nearly as artistic (or scary) as those in earlier times, the fact of their very appearance in the graveyard once again was striking enough.

One of the most telling of these later death's head stones is that for a sea-captain's wife, Dorothy Bickford Salter, who died in Portsmouth in March 1776, possibly, based on local folklore, due to worry and despair. Her husband, Captain John Salter, departed Newburyport, Massachusetts, in command of his ship *Crisis* in September 1775 in the early months of the Revolutionary War bound for Antigua, but was captured by a British warship and taken back to Boston, where Salter had his money stolen and was held hostage for some six months. On March 12, 1776, he was taken to Halifax, Nova Scotia, even further from his home and wife in Portsmouth, and put in chains aboard a prison ship. He was ultimately held prisoner in Halifax for seven weeks before being released, and after another three weeks' journey, finally made it home on July 16, 1776. Sadly, his wife, Dorothy, had died six days after he departed as a prisoner for Halifax, perhaps sick with despair over his fate. Her death's head-themed gravestone is indicative of not only the troubling times of the first years of the war, but also an associated personal loss.

By the 1730s, the long-used death's head motif had grown stale and no longer had the same visual impact, as the religious beliefs around ideas of salvation and the afterlife began to change, swinging markedly away from the dire beliefs of the early Puritans. This came about due to the advent of the extensive religious revival, known as the Great Awakening, which occurred beginning in the late 1730s in the Middle Atlantic colonies and New England. This revival spread in several waves, fueled by evangelist ministers like Gilbert Tennant and Englishman George Whitefield, and religion now became, for many, a joyous and happy experience, not one ruled by constant fear and doubt, and those ministers that preached this new faith, known as "New Light" ministers, gained many enthusiastic followers. Those who stuck with the old-fashioned Puritan beliefs, on the other-hand, were called the "Old Lights."

This Great Awakening changed New Hampshire attitudes greatly, and new gravestone motifs were just one small aspect of these societal changes. Now, the foreboding winged skulls became a thing of the past, entirely out of favor, though never completely disappearing. In their place, we see figures that are not skulls, but human-like forms, generally more pleasing in nature—some look like cherubs, others are more distinctly female or male in appearance, as well as some which are more gender neutral. These images are often termed "soul effigies," an idealized portrait of the soul of the deceased. Once again, figures like these were not just found on gravestones, but also in other decorative trades, including furniture-making and household décor. Indeed, it is clear that gravestone motifs changing with the times was little different, though in a slower-moving fashion, than the decorative arts and even modes of dress. What makes these soul effigies seem so radical and visually appealing, are the wide variety of facial expressions which they bear, symbolic of the wide range of emotions humans experience when we think of death. Some of these faces are sad, some angry, some ambivalent or anxious, while others are smiling happily and radiating joy.

As with any artistic creation, whether these gravestones embodied the ideals of the carvers themselves, that of their clients, or a combination of both is unknowable, but the later is probably most likely. Most interestingly, these soul effigies were not generally restricted by the gender of the deceased; there are plenty of examples of gravestones for men which feature distinctly female soul effigies, while there are also those found for women with a distinctly male soul effigy. One of the earliest of the soul effigy-type

Mary Batchelder, 1716, Pine Grove Cemetery, Hampton.

Dorothy Salter, 1776, Cotton Burial Ground, within South Street Cemetery complex, Portsmouth.

stones is that found in Portsmouth for Elizabeth (Butler) Penhallow. Dating from 1737, the soul effigy here is rather ambiguous in nature, both in regards to gender and emotional outlook. "Madam" Penhallow, as she was known, was the wife of Captain John Penhallow and was originally from Boston, where she first married merchant John Watts, who was a partner of John Penhallow. She first belonged to Boston's Second Church, but later moved to Arrowsic, Maine, with her husband and had several children. Captain Penhallow was there too, commanding the local garrison in this frontier town. The two surely knew each other well, as Elizabeth married Penhallow shortly after the death of her husband in 1717–1718, subsequently coming to Portsmouth.

Interesting examples of these soul effigies, which bear a somber appearance, include an early example in Pelham for a seven-day-old baby girl named Priscilla Chase, dated 1749, that for Hannah Cressy in Salem, dated 1763, which has the distinct appearance of a death mask, and that dated 1800 in Lempster for Rachel Hurd.

A more upbeat example of a soul effigy is that dated 1757 for Ruth (Hardy) Jewett in Hollis, one of the most pleasing examples to be found anywhere.

That in Hillsboro Center, dated 1798, for Elizabeth (Binney) Fisk, a native of Lincoln, Massachusetts, who moved here with her husband in 1782, depicts a face in a niche or alcove, complete with textured hair, staring coldly out at the viewer.

Elizabeth Penhallow, 1736/7, Proprietor's Burial Ground, within South Street Cemetery complex, Portsmouth.

Priscilla Chase, 1749, Pelham Center Cemetery, Pelham.

Hannah Cressy, 1763, Salem Center Burying Ground, Salem.

Left: Rachel Hurd, 1800, East Lempster Cemetery, Lempster.

Below: Ruth Jewet, 1757, Congregational Church Cemetery, Hollis. (*Courtesy of Beth Knoblock*)

Elizabeth Fisk, 1798, Hillsborough Center Cemetery, Hillsboro.

Stones of this design were the product of carver John Ball, a native of Hollis, New Hampshire, and are widely found throughout southern New Hampshire towns in and around the Merrimack River. Interestingly, this carver did have a gender bias in his work, documented by gravestone experts Theodore Chase and Laurel K. Gabel. Their studies reveal that Ball only carved these niched figures for women and children, while for men he carved a winged soul effigy with a face, which is ever so slightly more masculine. Why Ball carved his figures on gravestones for women and children without wings is unknown, but one explanation may be the fact that Christian theological interpretations for centuries had blamed women for the concept of original sin. The fall of Adam and Eve and their banishment from the Garden of Eden was put squarely on the shoulders of Eve, not on Adam, for while he willingly ate the apple Eve offered him from the tree of the knowledge of good and evil despite God's command not to do so, it was Eve who had been deceived by a serpent to eat the fruit in the first place, and subsequently offered it to Adam. However, the lack of wings was not the only gender identifier that this carver utilized, as some of his other works portray distinctly female figures, identifiable by either dress or body features. In Amherst, the highly stylized stone for young Martha Woolson, who died at the age of twenty-five in 1788, features a ruffled collar.

Not far away, in Paul Ball's hometown of Hollis, we find the stone for Rebekah Hardy, who died in 1792 "immediately after childbirth" at the age of thirty-two. Her stone may be interpreted as depicting either a woman in a collared dress, or perhaps showing the outlines of her breasts.

Martha Woolson, 1788, Town Hall Burial Ground, Amherst.

Rebekah Hardy, 1792, Congregational Church Cemetery, Hollis. (*Courtesy of Beth Knoblock*)

This may seem a bit odd for a gravestone, but the depiction of breasts in such carvings date back much earlier to the late 1600s and early 1700s. This was done in symbolic fashion, as is portrayed on the gravestone for young Mary Heath found in Seabrook. Mary, who was the daughter of Sarah and John Gove of Hampton, married a sea captain, Nehemiah Heath, and gave birth to eleven children between 1707 and her death in 1715 at the age of twenty-eight. It is very likely that she died due to the effects of childbirth after the birth of the couple's last child, a daughter named Mercy. While the main motif on Mary Heath's stone is a death's head, the side borders depict pendulous gourds, which clearly resemble breasts.

Such stones, which are the product of Boston area stonecutters whose works made their way into New Hampshire, have been heavily studied. Strangely enough, even the theology of the seemingly prudish Puritan theologians was somewhat obsessed with this aspect of the female anatomy. As historian Alan Ludwig documents in his book about Puritan gravestone carvings and their symbolism, Puritan divine Reverend Jonathan Edwards wrote that "Milk represents the word of God from the breasts of the church," while Reverend Thomas Hooker, first established in Boston and later founder of the Connecticut colony, stated more graphically that "that which makes the love of a husband increase toward his wife, is this, Hee is satisfied with her breasts at all times, and then he comes to be ravished with her love." Interestingly, Paul Ball was not the

Mary Heath, 1715, Elmwood Cemetery, Seabrook.

only gravestone carver to portray this aspect of the female anatomy, for another stone found in southern New Hampshire—that for Zipporah (Harris) Blake in Keene dated 1785—most certainly shows, without any ambiguity, a soul effigy with breasts. With such stones as these, we in the modern age are left to contemplate how such stones were chosen for these women. That they were socially acceptable is evident by the very fact of their placement in a number of towns, but just who chose them; was it the surviving spouse alone, or did he do so in accordance with his wife's expressed wishes, or did the women's sisters or daughters play any part in the decision-making process? Sadly, as with so many other details of life from the distant past, the answers to these questions can never be known. Interestingly, Zipporah Blake was married to town doctor Obadiah Blake and, in addition to bearing him seven children after their marriage in 1749, almost certainly assisted him in his medical duties, perhaps even taking care of minor medical issues when he was away on medical calls into Massachusetts and west into Vermont.

There is one other aspect of these soul effigies in the colonial era that also offers examples of gender identity, that relating to several aspects of female attire and appearance, headwear and hairstyle. For headwear, studies have shown that some carvers visually identified the female gender of the deceased by placing a bonnet on the head of her carved soul effigy, this being amply shown in the stone for Jane Greley of Pelham, dated 1762. The soul effigy on her stone, carved by Bradford, Massachusetts, stonecutter Joseph Mullicken, depicts a round face with a ruffled bonnet on top. While this detail was not always used on his carvings for women, his carvings for men always depict a bald-headed figure.

One final interesting stone that possibly depicts a hairstyle for a young girl is that for Mary Moulton of Hampton, who died at the age of three in 1753. While the curled designs on either side of the face of the soul effigy may be purely decorative in nature, they also offer the stylized appearance of a young girl's braided hairstyle. Once again, while the hollow and deep-set eyes of this stone are haunting to the viewer today, we can imagine that young Mary's parents may have taken some comfort in this unique and personalized detail. No matter what form they may have taken, the soul effigy style remained a staple motif in gravestone carving until it gradually faded away by the second decade of the 1800s, replaced in general by more traditional carved images of angels.

It should here be noted that, like the death's head, this motif seldom appeared north of Concord, except in the immediate Upper Connecticut River Valley where Vermont carvers predominated, as by the time the towns in this area were settled and well-established, the willow tree and urn motif had become the predominant favorite.

In addition to the soul effigies, another new type of gravestone that made its appearance beginning in the 1740s was the portrait stone. Unlike soul effigies, these were realistic portraits of individuals, men, women, and children, without overt religious connotations. The form might be waist length, showing an individual in period dress, or sometimes in the form of bust, representative of classical Greek and Roman statuary. In most cases, these portrait stones were not actual depictions of the deceased from real life, but rather may be classified as idealized portraits of the deceased, showing how they may have appeared in their youth. We know this to be true because the gravestone carvers/sculptors that crafted these stones sometimes used the same figure and mode of dress for multiple clients throughout New England, and the face of the same woman is therefore found, at least in the case of one carver, in places like Portsmouth,

Above left: Zipporah Blake, 1785,
Ash Swamp Cemetery, Keene.

Above right: Jane Gre(e)ly, 1762,
Pelham Center Cemetery, Pelham.

Right: Mary Moulton, 1753,
Pine Grove Cemetery, Hampton.

New Hampshire, York, Maine, as well as Boston. However, there are some portrait stones for young women that may be actual likenesses of the deceased. Because the faces on these stones are not repeated elsewhere, we can speculate that perhaps the likeness came from a portrait made of the deceased, whether in full size or miniature form, while they were still alive. This is certainly a possibility, given the fact that exquisite stones of the portrait type were much more expensive and therefore commissioned or procured by wealthy individuals with a high standing in society.

Indeed, in comparison to Massachusetts, colonial-era portrait stones are rare in mostly rural New Hampshire. There are only five examples I have discovered in my studies, three in North Cemetery in Portsmouth, which was our colony's wealthiest and most important town, as well as one in neighboring New Castle, and one in Concord. Three of these portrait stones are for females, one of whom was a young girl, as well as one for an adult male, and one for a male child, all of the deceased from wealthy and/ or influential families.

All of those examples in Portsmouth, interestingly, are for members of the Stoodly family, including young Elizabeth Stoodly and her sister, Mary (Stoodly) Folsom, who married in 1771. Their parents were Elizabeth and James Stoodly, who operated two well-known taverns in town, the King's Arms, and, after it burned down, the Stoodly Tavern beginning in 1761. Among the members of their household were two enslaved individuals, Frank and Flora. The Stoodley Tavern, now located on Hancock Street, is part of the historic Strawberry Banke Museum complex today.

It is interesting to note that for the female subjects, the portraits executed in stone generally match the age of the deceased in appearance, while that for Reverend Timothy Walker in Concord depicts a young boy, complete with a minister's collar. Of these New Hampshire portrait stones, the most detailed is that for young Abigail Frost in New Castle, who died in 1742 at the age of twenty-three. She was the daughter of one of the most distinguished men of the day in the area, the Honorable John Frost, who had been an officer in the Royal Navy and later was a wealthy merchant and member of the Governor's Council, while her mother, Mary Pepperell Frost, was from one of early Maine's most distinguished and wealthy families. Since this stone is a one of a kind it is highly likely that the bust carved here is an actual likeness of young Abigail. It is quite likely that the epitaph on her stone was written by her older sister, Sarah Frost Blunt, who is known to have written the epitaph carved on the stone of her husband, the Reverend John Blunt (died 1748), which is also found in the small Frost Family Cemetery.

The icons shown on young Abigail's stone highlight her religious beliefs, including the fact that "Hope" was the anchor of her soul, something Sarah Blunt would have known very well as both a sister and a minister's wife. It may also be that Sarah Blunt was the driving force behind the commissioning of this elaborate portrait stone for her younger sister, Abigail, who was the youngest of the ten Frost children and six years younger than her sister, Sarah. Portrait stones, though small in number, continued in use throughout the nineteenth and into the twentieth century. One of the most pleasing to be found is that in Fitzwilliam for Jane Felch dated 1858. Crafted at the height of the Victorian era, this stone features the face of a young woman in profile, complete with period hairstyle and the floral elements beneath that characterize Victorian-era gravestone carvings.

Above: Mary Folsom, 1784, North Cemetery, Portsmouth.

Right: Elizabeth Stoodly, 1757, North Cemetery, Portsmouth.

Above: Abigail Frost, 1742, Frost Cemetery, New Castle.

Left: Jane Felch, 1858, Village Cemetery, Fitzwilliam.

Sadly, Jane Holman Felch died of a "nursing canker," possibly the medical condition today known as "mastitis." An unusual and eye-catching late example is that found in Jaffrey for Dorothy Caldwell, who was the wife of a Danish artist named Viggo Brandt-Erichsen. Dorothy was from a wealthy family in Massachusetts who spent the summers of her youth in Jaffrey. She was studying art abroad in Paris when she met and married Brandt-Erichsen in 1924. The couple would have a child who died as an infant, followed by the death of Dorothy a short time later. Prior to her death, she had made known to her husband her desire to be buried in the beautiful town she had known as a young girl. Her husband subsequently honored her wishes by carrying the urns that contained the cremated remains of his wife and infant child from Paris and across the Atlantic Ocean to Jaffrey. Here he sculpted an unusual and striking tomb in her honor.

The tomb is well-known for its haunting portrait and the carved scenes of the Resurrection at the base, but is also interesting because Dorothy is memorialized under her own birth name first, rather than that of her married name. From this attribute, and the fact that Dorothy Caldwell was in Paris on her own, we can infer that she was certainly an independent-minded woman, her decision to study in Paris coming at a time when women in America had, finally, just a few short years before in 1920, achieved the right to vote.

Dorothy Caldwell, 1926, Old Burying Ground, Jaffrey Center.

Finally, while sculpted portrait stones were a manner in which the memory of the deceased, whether idealized or true to life, could be kept alive, the advent of the art of photography brought about portrait stones that featured actual photographic images of the deceased. Nineteenth-century examples that have survived the rigors of New Hampshire's weather cycles are very rare, but evidence of them can be found. Interesting remnants of examples, both for women, can be found in cemeteries in New Boston and Loudon, each featuring a limestone monument with an attached porcelain portrait holder, the portraits themselves either long worn away or somehow gone missing.

Later on, with advancements in technology, photographic portraits fired on ceramic became much more durable and by the early 1900s gravestones featuring portraits of the deceased became more readily available, especially in cities and towns with a large immigrant population like Boston. In New Hampshire, such stones are rare, that for Pauline Danceger Berlin in Portsmouth's Temple Israel Cemetery dating from 1920 being a notable example. This thirty-one-year-old Jewish woman was born in New York to Austrian parents and died of a pulmonary embolism, which occurred during an abortion procedure, the circumstances surrounding such being unknown, but probably due to complications during a difficult pregnancy. Pauline and her husband had an infant child who had died in March 1919 and is also buried here. She was married to Samuel Berlin, a Lithuanian immigrant who came to this country in 1902 and worked in Portsmouth as a house painter.

Paula Berlin, 1920, Temple Israel Cemetery, Portsmouth.

The last of the predominant motifs that were employed in colonial-era gravestone carving are those of the willow tree and urn, often used together, but just as often used on their own. Interestingly, neither of these motifs had their origins in America, but instead were imported here with the rise of the Neo-Classical movement, which was inspired by the rediscoveries of the ancient Greek, Roman, and Egyptian civilizations. This movement got its start in Europe from the mid-1700s, but by the 1760s was making its influence felt in America. This influence was not just seen in the graveyard, where these new motifs appeared and willow trees would come to be planted, but also in furniture design, wall and mural paintings, and even the needlework done by both young girls and older women alike.

In regards to the willow tree, it is not a tree that is native to America and was only imported here about the time that the gravestones that featured them also began to appear. Though many would soon come to associate the willow tree with death and mourning due to its bowed-down form, representative of someone prostrate with grief, its early influence likely came from the Bible, where the willow is mentioned several times in the Old Testament, perhaps most notably in Isaiah 44:4, where it is written that "I will pour my spirit upon thy seed, and my blessing upon thine offspring: and they shall spring up as among the grass, the willows by the water courses." The willow tree also has an association with Greek mythology, in particular with the goddess Persephone, the wife of Hades and co-ruler of the Underworld, where it is said that a grove of willow trees grew at the entrance to Hades. No matter its association, once the willow tree made its way into the iconography of New England gravestones, it would have a long reign, being widely used from the 1760s and throughout the nineteenth century.

As for the urn, while many today associate the urn with cremation practices, such funerary practices did not begin in America until the 1870s. The motif was instead inspired by ancient civilizations that did use funerary urns, the Greeks and Romans actually practicing cremation, while the Egyptians used these vessels in their embalming and mummification practices. Thus, the association of the urn with death has a long history dating back thousands of years, long before white colonists arrived in America. These urns, like the willows, came in many different forms and sizes, many of them topped off with an eternal flame.

Nice examples of willow tree and urn-themed stones include that in Dover for Elizabeth (Hovey) Mellen, dated 1793, and that for Elizabeth Warren in Bethlehem, dated 1797. Warren was the second person to die in the town of Bethlehem after Lydia Whipple (see below). She came here from Massachusetts with her husband, Jonas, about 1787 and gave birth here to a son named Otis, the first male child born in Bethlehem.

Throughout New Hampshire there are to be found a large amount of period gravestones that feature countless combinations of these motifs, often-times augmented with some of the older motifs more closely associated with death, including outlines of a coffin, and, on one very unique stone, the only one of its kind in the state, a standing skeleton. The combination of a skeleton, holding a staff in the form of the Grim Reaper, along with a central urn and a willow tree, is found on the gravestone for Mary (Purcell) Manning, who died in 1773 and is buried in Portsmouth's Pleasant Street Cemetery. Her husband, Thomas, was a well-known innkeeper in town, and Mary, herself the daughter of an inn-keeper, was undoubtedly a partner in that enterprise, but what inspired this choice of gravestone, crafted by Boston carver John Homer, is unknown.

Elizabeth Mellen, 1793, Pine Hill Cemetery, Dover.

Elizabeth Warren, 1797, Mount Washington Cemetery, Bethlehem.

Detail, Mary Manning, 1773, Pleasant Street Cemetery, Portsmouth.

Though the willow tree and urn stones would remain predominant in the post-colonial era and into the first decades of the nineteenth-century, by the late 1790s new gravestone styles were becoming accepted. Though professionally carved gravestones in the seventeenth and eighteenth centuries without a visual motif were outside the norm, by 1800 they were a common choice, perhaps a backlash to the symbolism of an earlier era that now seemed outdated. Indeed, many gravestones after this time for both women and men might feature elaborate lettering rather than any motif.

In those cases where motifs were chosen, many were seemingly more secular at first glance, but religious ideals were still underlaying factors in this art work. This was a time when floral elements beyond the simple willow tree would begin to make a more widespread appearance. Though still utilized in conjunction with the funerary urn in many cases, these floral elements were often executed in a vibrant manner, taking the willow tree to an entirely new level, or depicting entirely different forms of plant life altogether. For decades, these floral designs were used on the gravestones for both women and men, but by the late 1830s, floral-themed gravestones would begin to be used almost exclusively for women and children as the Victorian era developed. Early examples include that dated 1795 in Bethlehem for Lydia (Gates) Whipple, which features a pineapple, a symbol of welcome and friendship in colonial America, surrounded by swirling branches. Though damaged and badly worn, this stone is one of the finest pre-1800 carvings to be found in a northern New Hampshire cemetery. Lydia, who was probably born in Connecticut like her husband, Thomas, first lived in New Hampshire in Hinsdale, the couple and their five children subsequently coming to Bethlehem. Lydia was the first person, in fact, to die in Bethlehem, she having "sickened and it became apparent that she must soon bid farewell to loving friends."

Another beautiful early example is that dated 1798 for Elizabeth (Towle) Dearborn in Chester, which features a central urn with tulip finials, flanked by delicately carved tulip flowers on a long stem, with crossed branches below. The tulip is a rather late addition to New England gravestone iconography, one thought to be brought here by European immigrants.

The tulip motif was not just used because it was attractive, but also because it symbolized eternal life as tulips are the only flower that will grow after being cut. As floral symbols grew in popularity, countless designs, some stylized, some depicting recognizable flower types, developed. One common form was the six-petaled flower within a circle. This represented the so-called "flower of life," an ancient symbol that was sacred in many pre-Christian cultures and has been found on funerary art dating back to the seventh century B.C. in Europe. Its use on New England gravestones demonstrates yet another neoclassical influenced motif which had great appeal. That in Rindge for Alsa Brown, dated 1808, is a highly stylized and quite attractive example, while that in Claremont, dated 1814, for Meria Buckman is an attractive but more standardized version of the flower of life.

One related, plant-based motif that also became increasingly common in the nineteenth century was that of sheaves of wheat. Unlike most floral elements, this motif was typically used on the gravestones of older couples who had been married quite some time before their deaths. The symbol was a dual one, being representative of someone who had a long and fruitful life, but also had Biblical implications. Wheat is used to make bread, and Jesus stated that "I am the bread of life" (John 6:35), so wheat also represented the body of Christ and the Resurrection. Examples of this motif on gravestones are common throughout New Hampshire in various forms, those for Hannah (died 1888) and Walter Colburn (died 1884) in Newbury being nice examples. Hannah Dodge was married by her father to Walter Colburn, a farmer, in 1842, the couple married forty-two years before Walter's decease, and Hannah giving birth to ten children by 1863.

Gravestone iconography in New Hampshire and beyond in America reached new levels of importance and popularity during the Victorian era, beginning with the ascension of Queen Victoria to the royal throne in England in 1837 and lasting until her death in 1901. The attributes of this incredible period in history developed not just in England, but worldwide, including in the United States, where we have always had a fascination with old England's ruling family. The era has been heavily studied, written about, and documented in many different forms, but for our purposes several of its aspects were highly influential, their impact felt even in New Hampshire cemeteries.

First and foremost was the fascination with death and the mourning customs that were developed and heightened during the period, taken to new levels after the death of Queen Victoria's husband, queen consort Prince Albert, in 1861 at a young age. Afterwards, Queen Victoria was devastated and mourned the loss of her husband for a full five years and never got over her grief, wearing black for the rest of her life. Mourning customs involved the full scope of one's life in the Victorian era, not only inside the home, where mirrors were

Above: Detail, Lydia Whipple, 1795, Mount Washington Cemetery, Bethlehem.

Right: Elizabeth Dearborn, 1798, Village Cemetery, Chester.

Alsa Brown, 1808, Meeting House
Cemetery, Rindge.

Meria Buckman, 1814, Old Village
Cemetery, Claremont.

Hannah (1888) and Walter (1884) Colburn, Lakeside Cemetery, Newbury.

draped in black cloth and black clothing was worn for specified periods of time, but also outside the home, where public displays of grief, both within the cemetery and out, were common. Hitherto, the idea of decorating graves with flowers in New Hampshire and New England cemeteries would have been unthinkable, but this was no longer the case.

Indeed, unlike in old New England, appearances in and about the graveyard were everything and social status and one's family devotion were now on display in new and different ways. Not only were family plots, either enclosed with elaborate wrought-iron fencing or delineated with granite posts between which were often placed garlands of black iron chains hung with wrought-iron tassels, developed, but gravestones and monuments also reflected Victorian attitudes towards family and death. The era was one in which, with the rise of the middle-class, the family was now more important than ever.

The man worked outside the home, his wife responsible for homelife in general, where circumstances allowed aided by domestic help, including decorating the house and raising the children. Too, it was also an era of sentimentality and romantic love (the celebration of Valentine's Day as we now know it began in this period), this reflected in the many monuments that were erected for "Our Dear Mother" or "Beloved Father," sentiments that were mostly lacking on earlier New England gravestones. Most importantly, it was the Victorian attitude towards death that would change gravestone iconography. Death was largely viewed as a "passing," a journey from one stage of life to another, not as the grim affair that it often was, as was depicted by the grinning

Ames Family plot, *c.* 1830s, Old North Pembroke Cemetery, Pembroke.

death's head on colonial-era gravestones from an earlier age. Now, people did not die, they "passed away," or "fell asleep," or transformed from a bud on earth to a flower in heaven. These sentiments were held for all, but when it came to the gravestone motifs they inspired, some were used mainly for women and children.

The most common of these was the rose, a dual symbol of love and loss depicted in rosebush form, or sometimes as a single rose stem. Oft-times, the rose was shown in bud form, and other times in full bloom, but nearly always, especially when a death had occurred at a young age, in a drooped or broken form. This imagery symbolizes a life in full-bloom, cut short by death. One of the most outstanding of the early Victorian-era examples to be found in southern New Hampshire is that for Hannah Eastman Cotton in East Derry, who died in 1838 at the age of forty-four. This large stone, now broken and laying flat instead of upright, combines four different motifs, the most striking being the roses emanating from the funerary urns—because they are in full bloom and not in cut form, they are likely used here as a sign of love.

Of the other motifs on the Cotton stone, the hand pointing skyward was a common one in the era for both men and women, while the Angel Gabriel, in female form, calling the deceased to her maker was a common motif from the late colonial era, but one used by Victorians almost exclusively for women. It is no coincidence that such a striking stone as this was provided for Hannah Cotton, for it was carved in Exeter by a member of her own family, the Eastman name carved on the lower right portion of the stone. Of the cut-down rose type of gravestones, one nice example that is typical for that of a child, both girls and boys, who died during the Victorian era in New Hampshire is that in Bridgewater for thirteen-month-old Annabelle (spelled incorrectly on her stone) Batchelder dated 1864. Here we see the cut flower bud representing Annabelle, who died of diphtheria, lying on the ground.

A typical example for a grown woman is that dated 1869 for Carrie Butterfield, aged thirty-two, in Antrim. She was preceded in death by her young son, Willie, as is noted

Above: Detail, Hannah Cotton, 1838, Forest Hill Cemetery, East Derry.

Right: Annable Batchelder, 1864, Old Home Cemetery, Bridgewater.

on her gravestone. Note that the rose in full bloom, representative of Carrie, and the small bud, representative of her son, are drooping but not cut. Caroline "Carrie" Holt Butterfield, originally from Wilton, was employed as a dressmaker and died suddenly of apoplexy (heart attack or stroke).

In this same cemetery close-by is a similar, earlier gravestone for family member Mary Butterfield, aged six, dated 1847. Not surprisingly, other flower types were also commonly depicted on gravestones for women during the Victorian era, one of the most popular being the lily. It was popular not just for its religious symbolism and association with the Resurrection of Christ, but also the qualities of purity and innocence. A simple yet elegant example of the many that may be found in the state is that in Jackson for Helen Antoinette Dearborn, the wife of a farmer, who died in 1871 at the age of twenty-eight.

Of the other images used on gravestones for women during the Victorian era, one of the most popular was that depicting the human form in the guise of an angel, as opposed to the angel-like soul effigies of an earlier era. This was a comforting religious symbol that we today can easily understand. Remembering that for those in the Victorian era death was viewed as a passing from one life to another, better one, the angels depicted on period gravestones either facilitated that passage by carrying off the deceased, or were the end result, so to speak, of that passage, the deceased becoming an angel in heaven. A quaint example of the former type is that lovely stone in Exeter for Joanna Janvrin, who died in 1847 at the age of nineteen. Note that the angel here is holding the severed rosebud, while the banner above reads "Rest in Heaven." Regarding this young woman, we know little of her life or death.

An equally attractive yet more lifelike version of an angel for this type of stone may be found in nearby Kensington for Rebecca Peaslee, who died in 1852 at the age of forty due to erysipelas, a bacterial infection often caused by an insect bite. In this example, note that the angel is carrying a rose in full bloom and pointing skyward and next to a monument, which represents Rebecca's final resting place.

Interestingly, the Census of 1850 reveals that Rebecca Peaslee owned some $1,000 in real estate, $200 more than her husband, John, who practiced the trade of a shoemaker. A late example of the Victorian-style angel is that found etched on the monument for Ina Belle and Elsie Gile in Jackson, dated 1916–1918, the daughters of Vernie and Edward Gile. Ina Belle was a student when she passed away due to pulmonary tuberculosis, while Elsie died of meningitis. More elaborate angels that were carved in statuary form are most commonly found from the 1850s onward, both for young women, as well as for family monuments in general.

This type of monument not only characterizes the Victorian's grand attitudes in regards to mourning practices, but also, as has always been true in New England cemeteries, the wealth and status of the family involved. That for Miss Ada Smith in Lancaster, who "departed this life of consumption" in 1872 at the age of twenty-nine, is an impressive example of this style of monument, the winged-angel depicted with an anchor and broken chains symbolic of a premature death. Little is known of Ada, except that she was born in New Hampshire and was living with her mother, Annette Querry, also New Hampshire born and employed as a housekeeper, in Cincinnati, Ohio, by 1870, along with a young girl who was probably a step-sister, and no record of her father. It says something about a mother's love, determination (perhaps to honor her daughter's last wishes), and finances that she was able to bring Ada back to New Hampshire for burial and have erected this elaborate monument.

Above left: Carrie Butterfield, 1869, Maplewood Cemetery, Antrim.

Above right: Helen Dearborn, 1871, Village Cemetery, Jackson.

Above left: Joanna Janvrin, 1847, Winter Street Burial Ground, Exeter.

Above right: Rebecca Peaslee, 1852, Upper Yard Burial Ground, Kensington.

Above left: Ina (1916) and Elsie (1918) Gile, Village Cemetery, Jackson.

Above right: Ada Smith, 1872, Wilder Cemetery, Lancaster.

Another common human form carved on gravestones was that of an individual in a mourning or weeping posture. These are almost exclusively found on the monuments for women, but both male and female figures are found. That in Hillsborough Center for Miss Nancy Gilbert, who died in 1844 at the age of thirty-seven, is an exquisitely carved stone depicting a young woman, representative of Nancy Gilbert herself, weeping over a monument, on which is inscribed "Weep not for me, weep for yourselves." The directive in this imagery, coupled with her epitaph, is clear to the viewer: Miss Gilbert was now in a better place after suffering from a disease for seventeen years and her religion was what gave her the strength to endure. The stone for Susannah Platt in Kingston, who died in 1849 at the age of seventy-three, offers an entirely different perspective. Here, we see a male figure, representative of Susannah's husband, weeping over the grave of his wife. Such imagery, too, is completely in keeping with Victorian ideals, where public displays of grief were the norm and the patriarchal family structure on full display.

Yet another striking and charming form of Victorian era gravestones are those for children that depict an image of the child, often in a sleeping posture, or those featuring a mother and child together. As can be easily ascertained, this category of monuments is reflective of the prevailing attitudes towards death, where the deceased child is often characterized as having "fallen asleep with Jesus," as well as prevailing attitudes regarding motherhood. Indeed, while mother and child gravestone imagery are very prevalent throughout New Hampshire and New England, those depicting a father and his young child are largely nonexistent. The sleeping child monument comes in many artistic forms, but no matter how they are executed, they are both beautiful and striking to the senses. That in Atkinson for Eliza Frances Poor, dated 1860, is a simple yet elegant version, while that in Peterborough for Ella and Charlie Scott dated 1854–1857 is an emotional example of the monument-makers art with several underlying themes.

Since Charlie died in 1854 at the age of seven months, three years earlier than Ella, we are once again left to wonder how Charlie's grave was marked previously. The family, as will be seen later on with another family tragedy, was one of means, so it is likely that a monument of some kind previously marked Charlie's grave. As is clear, the death of Mary and Charles Scott's second child Ella within a short span of time not only occasioned deep grief, but the desire for a dual monument for their children.

Note that while Charlie's name is mentioned first below the sculptured images of the two children sleeping in each other's arms, it is Ella, who died at just three months old, who is depicted as the larger of the two sleeping children and clearly acting as her brother's comforter. Even in the death of an infant girl, the prevailing female role and ideal of providing comfort and care to children is upheld in period gravestone imagery such as this. Finally, the image of mother and child in gravestone art is one that has had a long history dating back to the soul effigy images of colonial times, often in conjunction with more stark images like the death's head and coffin. These images, however, were not always comforting ones, but rather a stark portrayal of the religious precepts of the day. The most famous of the colonial examples of this style of gravestone in all of New Hampshire is that for Lydia (Taylor) Worcester in Hollis, dated 1772. The stone's pair of skulls with crossbones flanking a single coffin tell a sad, and visually startling story about a woman and her unborn child.

However, during the Victorian era, the image of mother and child was, so to speak, resurrected in gravestone art in a more humanistic and appealing way. The gravestone

Above left: Nancy Gilbert, 1844, Hillsborough Center Cemetery, Hillsboro.

Above right: Susannah Platt, 1849, Plains Cemetery, Kingston.

Above left: Nancy Gilbert, 1844, Hillsborough Center Cemetery, Hillsboro.

Above right: Susannah Platt, 1849, Plains Cemetery, Kingston.

Lydia Worcester, 1772, Congregational
Church Cemetery, Hollis.

in Loudon for thirteen-month-old Susan Martha Marsh, dated 1856, the daughter of Martha and Courtland Marsh, features a comforting image of mother and child together, with the epitaph reading, in part, "Sleep on, my babe, thou loved and blest. I would not break thy peaceful rest."

Once again, the idea of "being at rest" was an important one not just psychologically, but also visually. In fact, many well-to-do Victorian era families had actual photos taken of their children after their death, either in a sleeping posture or in their parent's arms, to retain as cherished keepsakes of their little one, perhaps the only picture they had of their child.

There are three other Victorian era motifs that were commonly used for women and children, all of them having well-known religious connections and symbols just as comforting today as they were back in the nineteenth century. Perhaps the most common of these themes was the lamb, a well-known symbol of purity and innocence. This symbol was most commonly used for children, but was also used to a lesser extent for women. That for Mary Jane Clark in Dover, dated 1847, is a simple yet attractive version of such a stone.

The motif of the dove, sometimes in flight, sometimes at rest, was more popular than the lamb, especially for young women. This biblical bird is a symbol of innocence, peace,

Susan Martha Marsh, 1856, Loudon Center
Cemetery, Loudon.

Mary Jane Clark, 1847, Pine Hill Cemetery,
Dover.

and the resurrection, and when depicted soaring upward is representative of carrying the soul of the deceased to heaven. A beautiful version of the dove is that found in Chatham for Fanny Bryent, dated 1870, which depicts the dove carrying a broken bud in its beak, symbolic of a young life cut short.

Finally, there is the heart motif, which is also a dual motif, a symbol of love, but also a biblical symbol as the focus of one's body both physically and spiritually. This motif was used as a supporting element in colonial era gravestone art for the most part, used on stones for men and women alike and was even a common coffin lid decoration, but after 1800, the symbol of the heart was increasingly one that was depicted on women's gravestones, or chosen by a woman for her own family members. A simple yet beautiful early nineteenth-century example may be found in Cornish on the gravestone for Lucretia Wickware, dated 1815.

That in Enfield for Caroline Stowell, dated 1860, is an attractive example of a heart combined with the hand pointing skyward motif. Caroline Dutton was a native of Enfield who married Alfred Stowell in April 1859 and died less than a year later.

Finally, there are the materials from which gravestones and monuments were made, as well their overall shape and size. How these traditions changed over time also affected the gravestones for New Hampshire women, even if in subtle ways. Gravestones were first crafted from rough-cut stone that was locally available, but soon the grey slate

Fannie Bryent, 1870, Center Chatham Cemetery, Chatham.

Lucretia Wickware, 1815, Trinity Church Cemetery, Cornish.

Caroline Stowell, 1870, Follensbee Cemetery, Enfield.

for which New England gravestones are known was being used with the discovery of deposits on Boston's harbor islands and in other parts of Massachusetts. However, by 1800, new materials, including marble and limestone were being used as the quarrying and stone industry developed in northern New England. This resulted in finished gravestones that were a gleaming white in color, a marked departure from the dark-toned gravestones of the colonial era. Limestone especially was a much less expensive material and stones of this type could be produced anywhere, so they grew in popularity, their white color providing a perfect complement for the new motifs that emphasized such ideals as purity and innocence.

As for gravestones themselves, they first came in pairs, a headstone for the head of the grave, and a smaller footstone at the opposite end of the grave. The headstone, where most of the decorative carving was done, was first shaped like the headboard of an old-fashioned bed, having a rounded top, with rounded shoulders on either side. The footstone, which was of the same shape, had little in the way of decorative carving in most cases, it being common that the initials of the deceased were the only thing carved upon them. Because of their smaller size, many today wandering in old cemeteries mistake these for the gravestones of children. While unusually shaped stones have appeared in all time periods, the rounded-top gravestone shape would remain dominant until the late 1700s, when rounded top stones with square shoulders became the norm, and gravestones that were rectangular in shape, no longer resembling a headboard, began to appear.

Interestingly, several biases are readily apparent when it comes to the size of gravestones, especially in colonial times, but also in later periods. Indeed, the size of the gravestone or monument in any New England burial ground was an important and deliberate decision by surviving family members—not only are larger gravestones reliable indicators of the deceased's wealth and social standing in any given town, it was also often the case that when separate gravestones were erected for a man and his wife, that that for a man was larger than that for his wife. This was a clear indicator of New England's patriarchal society, and was a custom that lasted well into the first decades of the 1800s. An interesting example of this size bias may be seen in Goffstown for the side-by-side stones of Anna Ramsey Dodge (died 1812, aged eighty-four), and her husband, Antipas Dodge (died 1834, age 102).

While it is possible that Mr. Dodge was given a larger gravestone in deference to his remarkably long life, there are many other examples where this size difference is seen among men and women of roughly equal ages. However, it must be stated that there are also many other cases where a couple's gravestones are equal in size and even, albeit on a rarer basis, examples where the size of the woman's gravestone is markedly larger than that of her husband's. In cases like this, it is highly likely that this decision was made by the woman herself, or her surviving children. The old churchyard in Hollis offers up another example of size bias in the dual gravestone for Esther Kendrick (died 1775, aged twenty-two months), and her brother, Bowen Kendrick (died 1778, aged nine). Note that while the soul effigies for both children are the same, young Bowen's side of the gravestone is taller than that for little Esther.

This was no doubt due, at least in part, to the fact that Bowen was older, but a gender bias is almost certainly shown when we remember that male children in this time period were considered more important than female children, it being they that that would carry on the family name, and, as was customary, inherit the property of their father

Above: Anna (1812) and Antipas (1834) Dodge, Hillside Cemetery, Goffstown.

Left: Esther (1775) and Bowen (1778) Kendrick, Congregational Church Cemetery, Hollis.

upon his decease, sons often taking precedence even over their widowed mothers. It is also quite likely that after Esther's earlier death, no gravestone was erected by the family, her passing memorialized in stone only after the death of her older brother.

Finally, dual gravestones for a husband and wife that feature a size bias are less common, but can be found. That in Warren for Sarah Merrill and her husband, Stevens Merrill, dated 1804, is an interesting late example of this type of stone, which was by then out of style. Read just like a book from left to right, we can see from this gravestone that Sarah not only died first in 1791, but was also represented by the smaller half of the stone. Indeed, it is quite possible that in this rural community, Sarah had no permanent marker until after the death of her husband. Despite this fact, there is no doubt that she was well-remembered by all in this small community. Sarah and her husband, who were both from Newbury, Massachusetts, had ten children between 1752 and 1775, their last child, a daughter, Hannah, was born before the couple moved from Plaistow to Warren in 1775. We know little of Sarah's life in Warren, but she likely played a role in Warren's early school activities, as the first school in town was operated in the Merrill's barn, while later a private school was conducted inside the Merrill home.

Sarah (1791) and Stevens (1804) Merrill, Village Cemetery, Warren.

2

READING THE GRAVESTONE

Having discussed the symbolic aspects of gravestones, it is now time to turn our attention to the actual words carved on these stones. As interesting as the motifs of these period gravestones are, their epitaphs and inscriptions reveal to all, even the most casual observer, all sorts of fascinating details about the lives of women. Indeed, gravestones often offer a treasure-trove of information to the genealogist and historian alike, a tradition that, sadly, diminished over time, and was largely abandoned by the late 1800s, when fewer and fewer life details beyond name and years of birth and death were being preserved in stone. But, on earlier stones we can often read the exact age of the individual at death, broken down to the month and day, as well as the name of their spouse, children, or parents, and even the cause of their death in some cases. Other details that are often provided in these inscriptions and epitaphs are words describing the personal attributes of the deceased and their own views on religion, as well as their social status. However, the formula of these gravestone inscriptions and how they evolved over time right away shows a gender bias and the lesser status of women beginning in colonial society.

Early on, typical inscriptions for men would read something such as "Here lies Daniel Johnson, died December 13, 1697, aged 37 years." While commonplace occupations like blacksmith, farmer, or innkeeper were never noted on a man's gravestone, if a man held a military rank, or was a doctor, lawyer, or a minister, these titles were very often appended to their name on the stone. In fact, the higher their social standing, the more information about a man's standing is often found carved in stone. Very seldom is anything mentioned about their wives or children. However, on the gravestones of women and children, their position in the male-dominated society is almost always indicated by possessives. One interesting variant of this type of bias are those stones for women and children (of both sexes), which merely mention the first name of the deceased, a custom that lasted throughout the entire colonial period and was never used on the gravestones for grown men. An early example is the stone for "Anne, ye wife of George Jaffrey, Esq." who died in 1684 in Portsmouth just two weeks after the birth of the couple's first son. The couple was married in Boston, but it is unknown if Anne was a Massachusetts native, or, like her husband, a Scottish immigrant. A later example is that found in Charlestown for Hannah Holden, dated 1800, where she is simply referred to as "Mrs. Hannah, wife of Capt. Timothy Holden."

As can be seen, while women were almost always listed on period gravestones in possessive fashion, they also were often given the titles that defined their role or social status. The descriptors "wife" or "Mrs." were most common, but there were others that were used, some of which were archaic even in their time and thus are unfamiliar to many, while others are still common. Even during colonial times, the term "relict" was an ancient one, being defined as something, typically an object, which has survived from a much earlier time period. A carryover from old England, the term was most typically used to describe an aged widow. It is a strange term that harkens back to the deceased's time when she was married, and infers the fact that up to her death she was the surviving relict, the only object if you will, that is evidence of that marriage. The term was largely out of favor by 1800, but examples can be found in rural parts of the state for decades after, the term "widow" becoming more commonly used. For most of the examples found in New Hampshire, those women described as "relict" were aged seventy or above. The gravestone for Sarah Wood, a native of Newbury, Massachusetts, in Rindge dated 1790 is a fine example of this kind of work. Note that she first identifies as the former wife of Abner Spofford, with whom she had thirteen children during their nearly forty-three years of marriage beginning in 1734. After her first husband died in 1777, Sarah married Jonathan Wood of Boxford, Massachusetts, and lived in that town until his death, subsequently living the remainder of her years with her daughter Phebe in Rindge.

One of the most interesting of these "relict" stones is that in Amherst for Grace Towne. Her gravestone, a dual one she shared with her husband, Israel, was erected shortly after his death in 1791, and described her as "his Relict." Since Grace Towne was still alive when this gravestone was erected, it makes us wonder if she played any part in this decision as to how the couple's dual gravestone was designed and worded. Did Grace think of herself as a "relict", or did someone else, perhaps the stonecutter, decide on this archaic term? We know from town records that Grace was described as a "widow" and in her last years she was likely referred to as the "widow Towne" by those about Amherst. In fact, the term "relict" was generally, except in this case, not applied to a living widow. Interestingly, the inscription on her half of this soul effigy gravestone, as can be seen, was never finished. Grace Towne, according to Congregational Church records, died on September 6, 1803 at the age of about ninety-five, but it is a mystery as to why her stone was never completed. Possible explanations might include a lack of funds by surviving family members, traditional New England frugality, or even casual indifference as to details are all possible explanations for this lack of action, though one is left to wonder that, if circumstances were reversed, would Israel Towne's half of the stone have been finished, given his standing in town?

The appellation of "widow," the more common term now for a woman whose husband has predeceased her, was a common one in speech and, later in the colonial era largely replaced that of "relict" on gravestones. However, the term signified much more than we may think in an earlier time. While it is true that many women who became widowed in seventeenth- and eighteenth-century New Hampshire would marry again within a short period of time, often-times as short as a year, this was not always the pathway that a woman might choose.

Above: Anne Jaffrey, 1682, Point of Graves Cemetery, Portsmouth.

Left: Hannah Holden, 1800, Forest Hill Cemetery, Charlestown.

Sarah Wood, 1790, Meeting House Cemetery, Rindge.

Israel (1791) and Grace (1803) Towne, Town Hall Burial Ground, Amherst.

As historian Christine H. Tomsett has written in her article about widows in colonial New York, "Widowhood provided the greatest degree of freedom available to a woman in an age in which single women were controlled by their fathers and married women were dominated by their husbands." This included the economic freedom in New Hampshire and New England to own their own property (unless her inheritance was limited by her husband's will) and practice their own trade, usually that of inn or tavern-keeper. Thus, when viewing the gravestone for a "widow," we should not just think of that stereotypical image of an aged or elderly woman left to live a quiet life on her own after her husband's passing—far from it. Instead, we should imagine a strong-willed and determined woman who, upon gaining her stature of widowhood, found, perhaps, a new level of freedom in her life that she might never have dreamed possible.

There are many interesting examples of gravestones for women that were widowed several times over that can be found throughout New Hampshire. That in Lyme for Elizabeth Southworth, dated 1850, details her two marriages and notes the three marriages of her final husband, as well as the death of her father at the Battle of Bunker Hill in 1775, when she was just four months old. One gets the sense from a reading of her gravestone that Elizabeth Southworth was a strong and proud woman.

However, by the 1870s, conventions had changed yet again and the term widow was often dropped altogether, with women instead reverting to their maiden name on their gravestones while at the same time listing their deceased husband(s). One interesting example of the many gravestones of this type that can be found is that in Bethlehem for three-time widow Mary Batchellor dated 1871. This new standard was a distinct break in tradition with the practices in the colonial era, when gravestones conformed to English Common Law, where a married woman lost her legal identity upon being married.

This change was no doubt influenced by the rising women's suffrage movement and the establishment of such influential groups as the Women's Christian Temperance Union, which also worked to enfranchise women.

The term "consort" is another descriptor that is found on the gravestones of women that is somewhat confusing to viewers today. In modern terms, the term "consort" has a racy or illicit connotation that is suggestive, perhaps, of scandalous behavior. However, in old England, this term was actually used to describe the spouse of a reigning monarch, without regard to gender. In colonial America, this term certainly denoted the wife's subordinate relationship to the "reigning monarch" of the household, her husband. However, colonial literature also suggests that the term denotes in a more intimate way the close relationship between a man and woman who were not just partners in marriage, but also each other's best friends, confidants, and lovers. Oft-times the term "consort" is used in conjunction with the words "virtuous" and "amiable," to give an even better picture of the character of the deceased. Despite the fact that in its original use the term could be used to denote a male partner in a monarchy, in New England, it was never used to describe a woman's husband. It should also be noted, that unlike the term "relict," the term "consort" was used for women of all ages. The gravestone in Rochester for forty-five-year-old Betty Page, dated 1807, is a typical example.

Two other forms of address are also found on gravestones for women in New Hampshire. Of these, that of "Miss" was quite common, while that of "Madam" was less common. The term "Miss" was generally applied to young woman who deceased between the ages of eighteen and twenty-five, though it was also applied to older women

Elizabeth Southworth, 1850, Old Lyme Cemetery, Lyme.

Mary Batchellor, 1871, Mount Washington Cemetery, Bethlehem.

Betty Page, 1807, Old Town Cemetery, Rochester.

who were sometimes employed as schoolteachers. One charming example of this kind of stone, a fragment that dates from *c.* 1800, is found in Charlestown for Anna Pratt (age unknown), while one interesting example with a hidden story is found in Hillsboro Center for Betsy Kimball.

She died in 1831 at the age of twenty-two; at the bottom of her stone is the notation that this stone was "Erected by Josiah Crosby." Though uncertain, this man was quite possibly a suitor to Miss Kimball at the time of her decease, or at the least a very good friend.

While the use of the term "Miss" as a title for a young woman is most common, in other, more unusual, cases, it is stated in a more direct fashion. This is seen on the Watson family monument in Round Bay Cemetery in Laconia, where on one faded side is inscribed the name of "Emily Eliza Anna" with the brief epitaph "who died in young womanhood."

As for the term "Madam," this was decidedly one which was indicative of social standing and is most commonly found for those women who were the wives of town ministers, but also, in larger towns like Portsmouth, for the wives of wealthy merchants. Among the interesting examples that may be found in New Hampshire is that for Ruth Whitney in Keene, dated 1788, which describes this minister's wife's marriage to two men of the cloth, as well as describing her "Diligence, Patience, Piety, & Knowledge," and her characteristics as a wife, mother, neighbor, and Christian, indeed hitting all the categories and spheres of influence and interaction for women in that day and age.

Anna Pratt, ca. 1800, Forest Hill Cemetery, Charlestown.

Betsy Kimball, Hillsborough Center Cemetery, Hillsboro.

The very naming practices for female children in general from the last half of the eighteenth century and through much of the Victorian era, as well as the names which husbands and family members chose to have carved on their wives, daughters, and sister's gravestone are also telling of another type of bias that one seldom thinks about when wandering about New Hampshire cemeteries. Early names in the state for females, like the rest of New England, focused on strong Biblical figures, like Sarah, Ruth, Abigail, and Hannah, as well as names connected with the English monarchy like Elizabeth. However, as historian Gloria L. Main has documented, these naming practices changed as the times moved forward and religious ideals also changed after the 1750s, and female names became more casual, informal, and even infantile, based on diminutive names like Molly, Polly, Patty, Sally, Betty, Becky, and many others. Now, as Main states, "When these girls were to become adult women, they would still be addressed with children's names." However, for boys this was seldom the case and, as Mains writes, "the naming of sons remained a serious matter." These societal naming biases, of course, are on full display in New Hampshire cemeteries, based not only on what we see, but what cannot be seen. Diminutives like "Johnny" and "Billy" are not seen on the gravestones of grown men, but like examples for grown women abound. One interesting example is that stone dated 1804 in Francestown for Mrs. Becca Bixby, the thirty-nine-year-old wife of Thomas Bixby. The use of what may have been a husband's endearing name for his wife, Rebecca, is both charming and telling.

Would Mrs. Bixby herself have objected to this diminutive for her gravestone? It is on this question that historians and scholars need to be careful, and separate the overall gender bias practices of early nineteenth-century New Hampshire, which clearly existed, from the very personal interaction between married spouses. Possibly Rebecca Bixby would have whole-heartedly endorsed the shortened use of her name as a sign of her husband's love and affection. Another interesting example is that found in Seabrook for young Naby Brown, dated 1813, the wife of Lowell Brown. "Naby" is a diminutive for Abigail, but it is uncertain in this case whether "Naby" was her actual christening name, or just a nickname.

On the gravestones for men and women, when it comes to descriptive terms, there is a distinct dichotomy—for the regular guy—the farmer, the blacksmith, the mill worker, any descriptors on their gravestones are largely about describing their organizational affiliations, if they had any. The most predominant of these groups were the Masons, but later on, in the nineteenth century, this included other fraternal organizations like the Odd-Fellows. However, for women, professional and organizational descriptors were not possible until fairly late in the nineteenth century, and even then, are relative rarities.

For women's gravestones, then, it was all about describing their personal and religious characteristics, oft-times tied in with the medical conditions or physical disabilities they endured, often over the course of many years. In general, the wealthier or more prominent the family, the larger the inscription or epitaph that could be afforded if one was so desired. Examples abound throughout New Hampshire and can be found in almost every cemetery, though those examples from the colonial era are often the most elaborate and interesting. That for Mary Stinson in New Boston, dated 1798, is a simplified version of this style of gravestone, but makes its point nonetheless in succinct fashion, she described as "the sincere friend, the affectionate & virtuous Wife, The tender Mother, the patron of the Poor & the real Christian." Yet another fine example

Naby Brown, 1813, Elmwood Cemetery, Seabrook.

is that for thirty-nine-year-old Abigail Wilkins of Amherst, which focuses solely on her physical well-being, telling of her "Long & painful Sickness" and how she "Cheerfully resigned her Sperit [*sic*] into the hand of God," a point which is made abundantly clear by the soul effigies floating in the clouds at the top of her intricately carved stone. Indeed, words like "patience" and "endurance" are common ones on the gravestones for women, sure indicators that the lives of early New Hampshire women were seldom easy, even for those living in the best circumstances.

Finally, while such stones with these kinds of descriptors were common for grown women, even among young girls, these same ideals held true. The charming gravestone for six-year-old Elizabeth Halliburton, dated 1807, describes her as a "dutiful child." While the love that parents Elizabeth and Andrew had for their child is certainly evident, the curious choice of the word "dutiful" tells us that young Elizabeth was a well-behaved child who, perhaps more telling, did what she was supposed to do around the household. Was this choice of wording on her gravestone made by her mother or father? Though uncertain, it seems most likely that this word choice came from a mother's perspective.

While the term "dutiful" would be an odd choice today by any measure, it reminds us that in the early 1800s girls even at a young age were being trained for their future roles as housewives and mothers. While today we seldom think of housework as being dangerous, in earlier times the household tasks that were the responsibility of women, and their daughters when they were old enough to help, could sometimes cause injury

Mary Stinson, 1798, New Boston Cemetery, New Boston.

Abigail Wilkins, 1786, Town Hall Burial Ground, Amherst.

Elizabeth Halliburton, 1807, North Cemetery, Portsmouth.

or death. This was due to many common hazards, including the use of open fire for cooking, the dangers of open wells from which water was gathered, as well as that from being in the barnyard around large farm animals. This occupational hazard for young children is shockingly recorded on the gravestone for Patty Ward in Marlborough, who died in 1795, being "slain" by boiling cider, a once common method of preservation that results in apple-cider syrup, a foodstuff that will keep indefinitely.

One of the most interesting aspects of women's gravestones are those which describe in some fashion the relationship between a wife and husband. While in the later Victorian era, sentimental phrases such as "dear wife" or "beloved husband" are quite commonplace, those from the eighteenth century are most interesting, revealing a degree of deep personal relations that we do not often conjure up when we think of the traditional image of dour New Englanders and inscrutable New Hampshire folk. Interestingly, while the imagery on these colonial gravestones is often quite morbid, many of the personal inscriptions and epitaphs that accompanied them served to soften the message of death.

One of the most common phrases used on gravestones for married women after 1760 is that describing a wife as "amiable & virtuous." This phrase is an endearing one that certainly carried a personal meaning, but also likely has a wider influence. It is actually found in the writings of the Scottish economist and philosopher Adam Smith (1723–1790). While he is best known for his seminal work about the free-market economy, *The Wealth of Nations* (1776), his first major work was *The Theory of Moral Sentiments* (1759). This was a book in which he attempted to explain how man gained the ability to form moral judgements, with chapter five titled "Of the amiable and

67

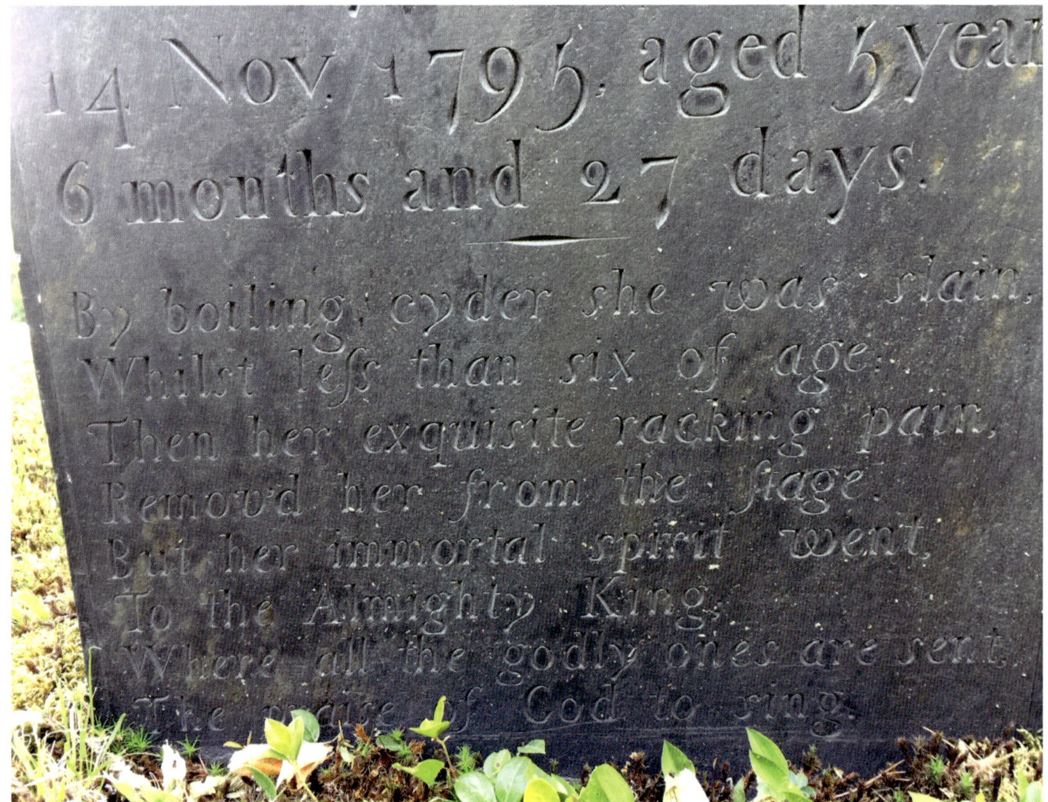

Detail, Patty Ward, 1795, Meeting House Cemetery, Marlborough.

respectable virtues." Here, Smith describes "the person principally concerned" and the "spectator" who is observing him or her and how they interact with one another. Though Smith's moral philosophy theories may seem like a strange gravestone influencer, in the frequently visited burial grounds of old New Hampshire, the interaction between the "amiable & virtuous" deceased woman (the "person principally concerned") and the spectator, be it family member, friend, or casual passer-by, who is reading her gravestone results in the spectator showing "indulgent humanity" and allows them to "enter into the sentiments of the person principally concerned".

Heady stuff for sure, but it is no coincidence that the term "amiable & virtuous" is most often found on the gravestones for the wives of New Hampshire ministers. These were educated men who would have been aware of Smith's work, the term "amiable & virtuous" serving to indicate the moral quality of their deceased wife. One such example is that in Greenland, dated 1785, for Mary (Montgomery) Macclintock, the wife of the popular town minister, Rev. Samuel McClintock, a graduate of Princeton University.

While the terminology of "amiable & virtuous" describes one aspect of a husband and wife's relationship, are there any gravestones that allude to the sexual relations between them? Strange as it may seem, even this aspect of relations between a wife and her husband can be found detailed in the cemetery, albeit examples of such in

Mary McClintock, 1785,
Hillside Cemetery, Greenland.

New Hampshire are exceedingly rare. However, the gravestone in Amherst for twenty-five-year-old Martha Dodge Kendall, the wife of John Kendall, dated 1801, does just that. On this lichen-obscured stone, there is the inscription, clearly written from the perspective of Martha's husband, which begins "This monument, erected by conjugal affection, is sacred to the memory of Mrs. Martha Kendall."

Clearly, the marriage bed for this young couple was an active and affectionate one, this inscription perhaps reminding us that our nineteenth-century ancestors, in some ways, were no different than us in the modern world. Martha, who was named after her mother, married her husband on August 23, 1799 and the couple had no children in the twenty-two months that they were married.

There are many examples where women exerted their will in the burial ground and cemetery, whether it be over the motif or wording employed on these gravestones, sometimes in the very fact that they were erected, as well as family groupings within the cemetery. In colonial times, women played a part in having gravestones erected, though how prominent of a one is open to question. This is clearly evident in Kensington for Joanna (died September 1775) and Ruben (died March 1776) Smith, whose final resting places may not even have been marked without the efforts of their daughter, Ruth (Smith) Lamprey. Their stones were almost certainly ordered at the same time,

Detail, Martha Kendall, 1801, Town Hall Burial Ground, Amherst.

coming from the workshop of nearby carver Jonathan Hartshorne in Newburyport, Massachusetts. At the bottom of each stone are the inscriptions, in big letters for all to see, "This for the respect Ruth Lampre had to her Dcst (deceased) mother" and "A gift for the respect Ruth Lampre had for her Dcst father". What is unclear about the ordering and placement of these stones is how they were paid for—was it through the funds saved by Ruth Lamprey and her husband, through money Ruth had earned and saved on her own, or with money she might have inherited from her parents? Whatever the case may have been, these unique stones make it clear that Ruth Lamprey had the idea of having these stones created for her parents, and followed through to get it done, and wanted everyone to know who had caused them to be placed, a sure sign of a determined New Hampshire woman.

Gravestones that show this level of involvement are rare for the time period, but as time progressed, women's involvement in having gravestones and memorials placed grew in frequency. An interesting later example of this type of stone is that for three members of the Mason family in Tamworth. Sarah Mason, the daughter of Tufton Mason of Tamworth, had erected for her great-grandmother, Mary Dalton, and grandparents, Elizabeth and Stephen Mason, a simple yet detailed gravestone sometime before her death in 1881. Though Sarah did not know her grandfather, she

Ruben Smith, 1776, Upper Yard Burial Ground, Kensington.

Joanah Smith, 1775, Upper Yard Burial Ground, Kensington.

knew her grandmother well, being fifteen years old at the time of her death. Since her grandparents were some of the first settlers in Tamworth, we can imagine that Sarah was captivated by her grandmother's story of how the family made their way from Hampton to Lake Winnipesaukee, making the crossing in a boat, whose sail was sewn by Elizabeth Mason, to Moultonborough.

Yet another woman who exercised her independence in the cemetery, albeit in a different manner, was Martha Cheswell (1788–1867) in Newmarket. She was the daughter of the renowned Wentworth Cheswell of that town, a man of mixed heritage, part black and part white, whose ancestor had been enslaved. Wentworth was born a free man and was well-educated, serving in an elite company during the Revolutionary War, and afterwards was man of letters who held office in several different capacities over the years, being the first black man to ever hold elected office in America. Cheswell's wife, Mary Davis Cheswell, was white, and most of the couple's children, including Martha, were also considered to be white. His youngest daughter, Martha, who never married, was considered a grand dame about town in her later years, and it was she who spruced up the family cemetery based on her father's wishes, having an elaborate wrought-iron gate made with her name and the year in which it was erected.

Her last will and testament decreed that the stone wall around the cemetery and its grounds was to be maintained by her descendants.

It is perhaps in regards to family groupings that women have had the most impact in the cemetery. While we do not know as much as we would like about how burial proximities were determined, there is enough anecdotal evidence in New Hampshire burial grounds and cemeteries to indicate that in some cases, whether it be those where widows decided which of their multiple husbands to be buried beside, where sisters were buried close to one another, where mothers and daughters were buried side by side, and where mothers and their infant children were buried together, that women played a major part in these decisions is clearly evident. Of course, the most common scenario to be found in any New Hampshire cemetery are those cases where wives and husbands are buried side by side. This was a situation that was determined by countless years of tradition, long before English settlers arrived here in early colonial times. However, it was not uncommon, especially if they were separated in death by many years, for wives and husbands to be separated in the burial ground in the colonial era. Indeed, old New Hampshire burial grounds are often places where family burial sites are scattered willy-nilly about the cemetery, close proximity among family members not always taking precedence.

However, after about 1820, with the development of the Rural Cemetery Movement, the idea of strictly delineated family plots came into vogue and would become the norm, family members often memorialized on a central monument or obelisk. From this time forth, the separation of family members was increasingly uncommon. This family separation in colonial times is most commonly seen in the case of widows, who at their decease were often buried, not beside their last husband, but an earlier husband. One of the earliest examples of this situation is found in Portsmouth, where, in 1711, Mary Keais (Keyes) was buried beside her first husband, mariner John Hoddy, who had died twenty-seven years earlier in 1684. Mary Riddan married John Hoddy in June 1675, the couple having four children between 1678 and 1683. The first born was Mary, their only daughter.

Right: Stephen (1800), Elizabeth (1820) Mason, and widow Dalton (1787), Riverside Cemetery, Tamworth.

Below: Martha Cheswell cemetery gate (1861), Cheswell Family Cemetery, Newmarket.

John Hoddy (1684)
and Mary Keais
(1711), Point of Graves
Cemetery, Portsmouth.

After Hoddy's death, his widow operated a tavern in Portsmouth between 1686 and 1694, later marrying Samuel Keais (Keyes) in 1696 and bearing two more children between 1697 and 1699. It is almost certain that Mary Keais was buried next to her first husband either due to her own wishes, or those of her daughter, Mary Hoddy Gerrish, who also figures strongly in the will of her stepfather in 1720.

Of course, the bond between mother and daughter is a strong one, and the precedence of that bond over the marital bond can occasionally be found. One of the most interesting of these examples is found in Kensington for Madam Elizabeth Parsons Fogg, her husband, Reverend Jeremiah Fogg, and Madam Fogg's mother, Elizabeth Parsons, who was the "consort" to Rev. William Parsons of nearby Salisbury, Massachusetts. Elizabeth Parsons died first in 1774, after having to come to Kensington to live with her daughter after her husband died. When Elizabeth Fogg died in 1779 at the age of sixty, after having been married for forty years, she was buried beside her mother. However, when Reverend Fogg died in 1789, he was buried beside his mother-in-law, not his wife, as was customary. Fogg had been the minister of Kensington for fifty-two years at his death, the town well-remembering in oral history the time when, in 1739, he brought his new bride to Kensington, she riding a horse and accompanied by Phyllis, her personal slave who was probably a wedding present. Interestingly, it may be that Phyllis Fogg is buried in this same cemetery, but, if so, her final resting place is unmarked.

The bonds of sisterhood are strong ones, and they make their appearance, too, in the cemetery in a sometimes unique and interesting manner. Of course, sisters grow up, get married, and even if they remain close geographically speaking, as well as in their relationship with

Elizabeth Parsons (1774), center, Elizabeth Fogg (1779), left, and Jeremiah Fogg (1789), right, Upper Yard Burial Ground, Kensington.

one another, they are usually buried apart, especially if married or their deaths are separated by a wide space of time. However, for twin girls, just as they were close in life, so too are they often close in death. The dual gravestone for Ella Jeannette Nichols Little (died 1871) and Estelle Jane Nichols (died 1872) in Hampstead is quite interesting, the twin girls memorialized together, this bond of equal importance, perhaps even more so, than Ella's marriage.

Of these young women, we know little, including how they died, or their life details, except that Ella Little had one daughter, Jessie, who was born in 1867. Likewise, not far away in Atkinson is the gravestone for twin sisters Lydia and Sarah Richards, who died within a week of each other in May 1868. In this case, both were aged; one, Sarah (referred to as "Sallie" in death records), a spinster, the other, Lydia, had been married, but was a widow for the last twenty-nine years of her life, the two women likely living together.

Not surprisingly, dual gravestones, or even single gravestones that denote this status, for twin brothers who are grown are fairly rare.

While all of our previous discussions regarding gravestones have focused on those for white women, it will be here appropriate to talk about those for women of color in New Hampshire, both enslaved and free. Sadly, inscribed markers for African American women in the state prior to 1800 are non-extant, while for African American men only one is known to exist. In Seacoast area towns like Portsmouth and Exeter, where free-Black populations existed, most did not have the economic means to purchase professionally carved grave markers and instead likely used simple fieldstones. As for the enslaved, the few that were provided with any grave markers, like the Langdon family slaves in Portsmouth, were given simple fieldstone markers too, without inscriptions of any kind.

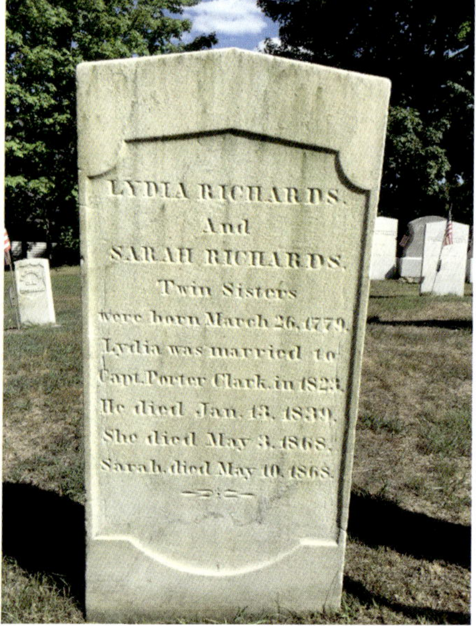

Above: Ella Little (1871) and Estelle Nichols (1872), Hampstead Center Cemetery, Hampstead.

Left: Lydia and Sarah Richards, 1868, Old Atkinson Cemetery, Atkinson.

There was once a separate "Negro" burial ground in downtown Portsmouth prior to 1800, but there is no evidence that the site on Chestnut Street, now the Portsmouth African Burying Ground Memorial Park, ever contained any professionally carved gravestones. From 1800 onward, grave markers for African Americans in New Hampshire begin to appear, though they are still relatively rare between 1800 and 1850; however, after that time, the numbers, though still low compared to the white population, do rise. Those grave markers which are found from 1800 onward are identical to those for whites when it comes to the motifs used. This is not surprising, as African Americans were not employed in the stone-cutting busines, just like most of the rest of New England (except for one African American stonecutter documented in Newport, Rhode Island). Most of the time, too, their inscriptions and epitaphs follow the same conventions as gravestones for whites. However, there are gravestones for two New Hampshire women of color that are of great interest.

The first of these is found in Franklin for Silva Marcy Kimball, "the faithful servant" of the Thompson family who died in 1800 at the age of fourteen. Silva was in fact the slave of the Thompson family, the term "servant" a rare one in New Hampshire, but common elsewhere in New England as a euphemism for "slave."

Her professionally carved gravestone, indeed indicative of the affection the family had for Silva, was procured from a carver in Newburyport, Massachusetts, a town with close ties to the slave trade, one of the Thompson family from that town a merchant dealing with the southern tobacco trade. Silva Marcy's stone is an important artifact in New Hampshire, tangible evidence that slavery existed in New Hampshire in rural places far from the Seacoast area even into the nineteenth century.

Our other stone of note is that for Violate Fortune, the wife of Amos Fortune, who died in 1802 in Jaffrey. The markers for her and her husband are well-known, without a doubt the most famous and visited grave markers for early African American residents in the state. Amos Fortune was born in Africa and brought to America as a slave. He was living in Woburn, Massachusetts, and was supposed to have been freed within six years of his master's death in 1752. However, the provisions in his master's will were not honored by his heirs, and Fortune remained a slave before he finally paid for his freedom in 1770. Desirous of a companion, Fortune freed his first wife by purchasing her from her master, but she died within a short time. Fortune's second wife was Violate, whom he courted and subsequently purchased from her master in Woburn for fifty pounds, and married her the very next day. The couple would subsequently move to Jaffrey in 1781 and lived out the remainder of their years free, Amos practicing the trade of a tanner, while Violate tended to their home and cared for two young African American women that came to live with them from about 1785 onward. Violate's beautiful gravestone is an interesting one, especially for the epitaph, which was written not by the Fortunes, but by a white church deacon who offered his own unique and legalistic (perhaps) view on the Fortune's relationship, stating that Violate was "by sale the slave of Amos Fortune," her husband. This gravestone takes the tradition of mentioning women in possessive fashion to the extreme, and it is hardly likely that either Amos or Violate would have approved of such a sentiment.

Finally, while New Hampshire cemeteries and the gravestones within them speak to family relations both directly and indirectly, there is no stronger or poignantly demonstrated bond than that of mother and child. Gravestones that demonstrate this

Silva Marcy Kimball, 1800, Webster Lake Cemetery, Franklin.

Violate Fortune, 1802, Old Burying Ground, Jaffrey Center.

bond come in several forms, as has previously been shown, where motifs, inscriptions, or a combination of both, serve to tell us a story. However, there is one type of gravestone that was abundant in colonial-era New Hampshire and all of New England, which later fell out of favor, these being ones that show the tragic turn of events which took place during childbirth.

Viewing the stones that mark the tragic passing of a newborn child, mother, or both is startling to us today, but was an all-too common event in earlier days when medical science had yet to be developed. However, even though our ancestors had to accept tragic events like this as a part of life, that does not mean they did not feel pain and anguish at these losses. Indeed, because of the large families that existed in colonial times and later, we in the modern age often have the mistaken notion that they, perhaps because of their stoic religious beliefs, accepted what came to them and grieved in a different or lesser way than we might. In fact, gravestones in this category often paint a much different picture. The gravestone in Hollis for Mary Jewett and her two infant children, dated 1816, offers us the timing of her death in stark simplicity.

Likewise, that in Portsmouth for Mrs. Salley Sherburne and her eighteen-hour-old daughter, Salley, dated 1787, does the same, telling us of an expectant couple who had already chosen a name for their child.

Mary Jewett, 1816, Congregational Church Cemetery, Hollis. (*Courtesy of Beth Knoblock*)

Salley Sherburne (1787) and infant Salley Sherburne (1787), Cotton Burying Ground, South Street Cemetery complex, Portsmouth.

Oft-times, the infant child, however, went unnamed on the gravestone, including the "stillborn Babe" buried on the arm of twenty-one-year-old Prudence Osgood in Claremont in 1812, and the "little Babe" of Rebekah (Paige) Cutler in Rindge. She died from the effects of childbirth at the age of forty in 1782. Rebekah was a native of Bedford, Massachusetts, who was married to her husband in neighboring Lexington two days before Christmas in 1761. The couple moved to Rindge about 1771, and had eight children, all but one of which (the "babe" listed on her gravestone) grew to adulthood. Rebekah not only raised a large family, but was almost certainly an integral part in her husband's activities as an innkeeper.

While these examples are typical of this type of gravestone that was prominent from colonial times into the 1830s, that in Orford for Lydia Dewey, dated 1784, is somewhat more unique. Not only does it mention specifically that she "died in Childbed" and was buried with her son "on her Right Arm," but it also offers an epitaph from the perspective of her newborn son, which reads "My Sister & I in Childbed died & here we lie both Side by Side." While the records are unclear about this family's children, the epitaph implies that this stone actually represents a triple burial, that for Lydia Dewey and her twin children.

Above left: Prudence Osgood and child, 1812, Old Village Cemetery, Claremont.

Above right: Rebekah Cutler and child, 1782, Meeting House Cemetery, Rindge.

Right: Lydia Dewey and children, 1784, West Cemetery, Orford.

3

THE CHANGE TO MODERN MONUMENTS

The traditions surrounding gravestones that started in early colonial times, as we have seen, gradually changed over the centuries. Obelisks and statuesque monuments, though rare, started to make their appearance by the end of the eighteenth century in New Hampshire cemeteries. By the first decades of the nineteenth century, the concept of the multi-generational family plot, delineated by elaborate enclosures that marked the family's space as their own, became more common, but most still featured individual gravestones. However, by the 1850s, the concept of the central family monument had become more widespread and, as can be seen in such city cemeteries as Manchester's Pine Grove Cemetery, and Blossom Hill Cemetery in Concord, individualized gravestones became increasingly rare.

This change was brought about by several factors, the first being, quite simply, the changing times and tastes in mortuary customs brought about by the Victorian era. However, the growth of industry and rail transportation on a broader level also spurred change. This is particularly true in regards to the granite quarrying industry in Concord and elsewhere in the state. Just as in other locales in New England, like Quincy, Massachusetts, and Barre, Vermont, the rise of this industry changed the gravestone, now monument, trade from one that was highly specialized to that of a regional trade where the end provider was not the primary craftsman. Now, nearly every town of any size had a monument dealer who could provide burial markers that had already been finished except for the personal details. Indeed, when a family had attained some measure of economic resources, it was common practice in a family plot to remove individual gravestones, these often being sold to those in the building trades as paving, flooring, or foundation stones, and replace them with a central monument which listed all the family members buried here. Indeed, if you have ever owned an older home in New Hampshire, and turned over a slab of stone, perhaps in a basement during renovations, only to find that it had once been used as a gravestone, now you know why.

It is interesting to note that individualized inscriptions and epitaphs from earlier individual gravestones were rarely replicated on new family monuments. In fact, with the gradual change from individualized gravestones to family monuments, information that had once been commonplace on a gravestone was no longer supplied, such details having fallen out of favor, and in the vast majority of cases, burial markers became more impersonal for all members of the family. However, for women, whose stones were already less personalized than those of men, this change in tradition resulted in a further loss of identity. Monuments were most often procured when the patriarch of a given family died, the monument bearing the family's last name, but also at times any affiliations the patriarch may have had, including fraternal organizations like the Masonic Order or the Odd Fellows, as well as those associated with military service, especially for Civil War veterans.

In general, while maiden names for married women were still commonly listed on these monuments, little information beyond years of birth and death were provided. Additionally, it is not uncommon to see examples of monuments manufactured from the late nineteenth century down to modern times where a woman's year of death is omitted, including those for Ruth Ferris Corey and Elizabeth Ann Virgil (see Part II), making their life details even more vague. While missing death dates can also be found on monuments for male family members, this is most commonly found for sons who were perhaps of a younger age when a monument was placed and their name and year of birth inscribed, they subsequently moving to another locale and perhaps were not even buried in the old family plot upon their decease. As to the missing death dates for women, this could have occurred due to many factors, one of the most obvious being the fact that by the late nineteenth century, the average life-expectancy for women outpaced that for men, a situation that continues to this day. Thus, we know that in some cases, not only did married women take care to ensure that their husband's final information was recorded, but upon their deaths, there may have been no close family member remaining to do the same for them. In other cases, aged women may have lived the last years of their life with a son or daughter, perhaps in another town altogether.

Finally, though the change to family monuments often resulted in a loss of identity, this was not always the case, and there are a number of interesting monuments for woman, including several whose lives are discussed in Part II, to be found in New Hampshire. That in Keene for educator Catherine Fiske is an early example, while that in Concord for former Army nurse Harriet Dame is an unusual example with a military theme. Both of these women were unmarried, and so it is no coincidence that these monuments are reflective of their individual achievements.

One of the most striking, and enigmatic of these monuments may be found in Dover's Pine Hill Cemetery for Cordelia Teatherly, who died in 1891. The circumstances surrounding her death are uncertain, but legends abound in town that state that Cordelia, who had previously been widowed, was engaged to Henry Law, one of the town's most prominent citizens. It is said that he broke off an engagement with Cordelia because he did not like her pet dog and she refused to get rid of it. Cordelia subsequently committed suicide, hanging herself, it is said, due to a broken heart. At her death, she left a diamond ring and some railroad stock to Law, who was single his entire life and is buried in the plot next to hers with a large monument. It is thought that Henry Law possibly bought the cemetery plot for Teatherly, even though there is no record of this, as well as the monument itself. The monument features a sitting woman with head bowed down—perhaps she is thinking, or maybe she is crying, but locally the monument is known as the "weeping bride." It is also pointed out that the woman is looking away from the site where Henry Law was buried in 1938…is this a mere coincidence? No one really knows.

Cordelia Teatherly, 1891, Pine Hill Cemetery, Dover. The monument for Henry Law is at far right.

PART II

GRANITE WOMEN

In this section, we will examine the lives of forty-one notable women who are buried in New Hampshire cemeteries. My criteria for the selections made here was fairly simple: the women in question had to have an identifiable grave site and gravestone, and while being native-born was not a requirement, having a tangible connection to the state was. The choices I had hoped to make did not always go as planned, leading to some unfortunate exclusions, while of the other choices that have been made, there will inevitably be some readers who wonder why this particular woman or that was excluded or included. It is my hope that the reasons for the choices I did make will be made clear and evident. In reality, this work is far from being a definitive one, as there is way too much ground to cover, so to speak, even in this small state. Instead, I like to think of this work as a sampler, or starting point, if you will, for future story-tellers, whether by myself or other historians, writers, or cemetery ramblers who are willing to search out the many stories of Granite women still waiting to be told.

4

FRONTIER WOMEN

The lives of women were incredibly difficult in early New Hampshire, even for those who were from relatively wealthy families. Not only were there occupational hazards from everyday domestic life, but also those resulting from the efforts required to establish a home in the wilderness and even the danger of Indian attacks into the 1750s. New Hampshire women had to be strong and independent—not only did they often bear many children and raise large families, but they often were the sole protectors and caregivers of their family when their husbands were away from home, perhaps foraging in the wilderness or gone off to larger towns to obtain needed provisions and supplies. Indeed, there are many accounts in town histories of women who manned local garrisons, or had to know how to use a musket to fight off bears and other wild animals. Of most of these women, we know little, beyond the names of their parents, husbands, and children, but of a few there can be found extra details of their lives and, in some cases, tragic deaths.

ELIZABETH ELATSON (C. 1659–1704) AND ELIZABETH ROGERS (1703–1704), POINT OF GRAVES CEMETERY, PORTSMOUTH

Born Elizabeth Pemberton, Elizabeth Elatson was first married to George Purkis (widowed in 1682), and then Warner Wessendonk (widowed 1690). She then married a Boston merchant named Jonathan Elatson in 1695, but their time together was short, he dying by 1697. Jonathan Elatson was well-off, involved in the West Indies trade, and even acquired for his wife a personal slave. Elizabeth Elatson had only one known child, a daughter named Sarah Purkis, who married Rev. Nathaniel Rogers, a native of Ipswich, Massachusetts, and graduate of Harvard in 1687. After preaching at Salem Village in Massachusetts, Rev. Rogers and his family, including his mother-in-law, Elizabeth Elatson (and her female slave), came to Portsmouth in 1699. Elizabeth likely helped her daughter care for her older grandchildren, Nathaniel, Jr., and Sarah, and was surely pleased in 1703 when the newest addition to the Rogers family was named in her honor. Sadly, their time of happiness after this event would last but seventeen months.

On the evening of October 30, 1704, the Rogers' house caught fire and burned to the ground. The fire likely started in the kitchen but spread quickly to engulf the timber-framed house, the flames spread by strong winds. Elizabeth Elatson in her upper story bed chamber was able to get to her oldest grandchild, Nathaniel, and threw him out the window to his father below, and was subsequently rescued by the reverend who was able to bring a ladder to her window. Lost in the fire was young Elizabeth Rogers, as well as Elatson's slave woman (who is not named and whose place of burial is unknown). Elizabeth Elatson was badly burned on her legs and arms, but it was thought these burns were not fatal. However, this did not prove to be the case, and after lingering for two months, she finally succumbed to her burns and was laid to rest beside her granddaughter, a dual gravestone marking their final resting place being obtained from a Boston-area carver. We only know about this event in detail because it was the first house fire in the colonies to be reported in the first American newspaper, the account appearing in the *Boston News-Letter*, dated November 6, 1704.

ELIZABETH BURNHAM (*C.* 1701-1724), OLD PARISH CEMETERY, LEE

Elizabeth Burnham was the youngest child of Lt. Jeremiah Burnham and his wife, Temperance Bickford Burnham. The family was a prominent one in Dover, a portion of which town was later set off as the town of Lee. The family lived in a type of dwelling known as a "garrison house" (one of many in this frontier town), it distinguished by its strong timbers and loopholes in the wall, which allowed for those inside to shoot at intruders outside. In the years before Elizabeth Burnham was born, the Burnham garrison house was even manned by two soldiers for a time. The first decades of the 1700s was a time of intensifying Indian raids, with the town of Dover largely abandoned in 1719 due to them. Young Elizabeth Burnham was wounded during a subsequent Indian raid on May 24, 1724 while returning home from services at the meeting house.

Town lore reported by historian Mary Thompson states that she had been returning home in the company of her lover, but the facts surrounding this cannot be ascertained. Gravely wounded, Burnham's bloody handprint was left on a boulder in the vicinity of the attack. Four days after the attack, Elizabeth Burnham died of her wounds, town legend also stating that the night before her death she was "penitent" and requested of Rev. Hugh Adams that she be baptized. The boulder upon which Burnham lay wounded, according to tradition, remains in the Old Parish Burial Ground today where she was laid to rest, said to forever be stained a reddish-brown color by the blood that was spilled upon it. While there is a reddish spot upon the rock which is faintly visible to today's visitor, it is unclear if this is just part of the rock's composition or really is an ancient bloodstain.

Whatever the case may be, the boulder at her gravesite, at the very least, is symbolic of the real dangers faced by the early settlers here. One may even wonder if Elizabeth Burnham herself was trained to fire a musket—quite likely she was, being the daughter of a soldier-citizen who lived in a time of constant danger and might be required at any time, day or night, to help in manning their garrison house. Elizabeth Burnham's marker, as noted from its inscription, was placed in the early twentieth century, and it is likely that prior to this time her grave had no professionally carved gravestone, as was the case with other early residents.

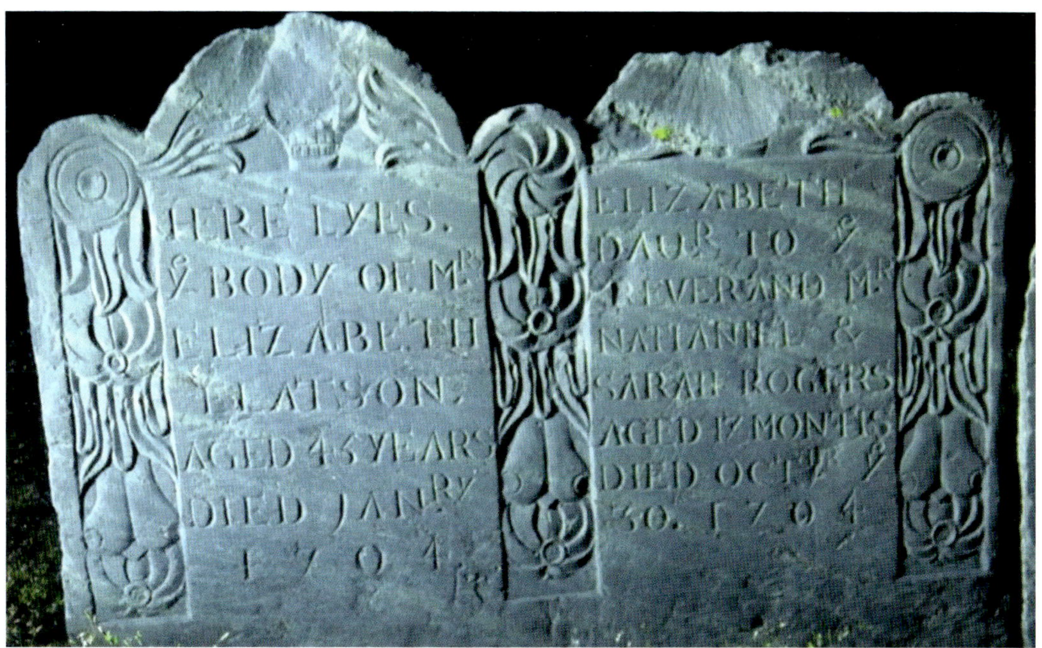

Above: Elizabeth Elatson (1704) and Elizabeth Rogers (1704), Point of Graves Cemetery, Portsmouth.

Right: Elizabeth Burnham, 1724 (placed 1907), Old Parish Cemetery, Lee.

CHRISTIAN MCNEIL (*C.* 1687–1753), VALLEY STREET CEMETERY, MANCHESTER

Quite simply, this gravestone is one of my favorites, for the fact that the woman buried here is representative, I think, of the hardy Scotch-Irish immigrants who first settled this part of the state beginning in the early 1700s. We only know a few things about her, they coming from Manchester historian C.E. Potter. The first is that she was the wife of John McNeil, who came to Londonderry from Ireland in 1719, forced to emigrate after "attacking a person of distinction" in his home neighborhood, even if the cause was justified. So, John McNeil, a man who stood 6 feet 6 inches tall, came to New Hampshire, his wife, Christian McNeil, herself "of strong frame and great energy and courage," by his side. John McNeil soon enough gained a reputation in New Hampshire for his strength, courage, and skill as a wrestler, and few "dared to risk a hand-to-hand encounter with him."

Lore states that one day, while he was away from home, a man came to the McNeil home, and when Christian McNeil told him her husband was away and asked his business, the disappointed man said he had heard of John McNeil's strength and skill and had come some distance to "throw him." Well skilled to keep up the McNeil family reputation, Christian is said to have replied to the stranger "An troth mon … Johnny is gone, but I'm not the woman to see ya disappointed, an' I think if ye'll try mon, I'll throw ya meself." Not liking to be taunted by a woman, the man accepted Christian McNeil's challenge, whereupon she quickly tripped him up and "threw him upon the ground." The stranger quickly departed, his tail between his legs, too embarrassed to leave his name.

Christian McNeil was no doubt a woman of strength, courage, and good humor as well, a strong partner in her marriage to John McNeil. The couple lived in the area of Amoskeag Falls in what is now Manchester, John possibly employed as a ferryman,

Chresten McNeil, 1754, Valley Street Cemetery, Manchester.

manning a canoe near the falls and charged with keeping safe those who fished there. Interestingly, for years one of the rocks in the Merrimack River near the falls was nicknamed "Old McNeil," as John McNeil had fallen through the ice in the wintertime and used the rock and his "superhuman" strength to save himself from drowning. Christian McNeil was originally buried on the family farm near a brook that bore her name, Christian's Brook, and when later on this land was taken over by the Amoskeag Manufacturing Company, the remains in the Christian's Brook Cemetery, at least those that were marked, were moved into the Valley Street Cemetery.

Susannah Willard Johnson Hastings (1730–1810), Forest Hill Cemetery, Charlestown

If one needs any proof of the resilience of the New Hampshire frontier woman, they need look no further than this incredible individual, who endured trials and tribulations that few in the modern world can even imagine. Susannah Johnson was born in Lunenburg, Massachusetts, and first came to New Hampshire in 1744, when she visited Fort #4, Charlestown, to be with her family, having travelled "through the gloomy forest," as she would later recall. The inhabitants at Fort #4 were few, it having been established just four years earlier, and on entering the settlement one of the first things she saw was a party of Indians performing a war dance. It was to be a prophetic sight.

Susannah would subsequently marry a soldier, Captain James Johnson, in her hometown in 1747, and two years later, with the peace between Great Britain and France signed and Indian depredations on the New Hampshire frontier apparently over, the couple moved to Charlestown. The peace was an uneasy one, but James Johnson would eventually move his family to a farm outside the fort and here the family prospered. However, with war on the horizon looming again in 1754, the safety of the settlement was now more precarious. Susannah, left at home pregnant and alone with her children, including six-year-old Sylvanus, was deeply worried but gained relief when her husband returned home from a trading expedition on August 24. That relief was but temporary, as Indians invaded Fort #4 in the early hours of August 30, a war party bursting into the Johnson home and taking the family, including Susannah's sister, Miriam, and a neighbor man, captive.

Susannah and her three children were naked, finally being allowed some light clothing, before being marched out of the house to begin a journey through the New England wilderness to Canada. Here, the Indians would profit from their raid by selling their captives to the French at Montreal, a common practice during wartime in colonial New England. The overland journey to Canada took three weeks, Susannah travelling at first on foot, then on a captured horse, and later carried by her husband. It was a harrowing journey for even the stoutest man, but in her pregnant state, it was even more difficult. Incredibly, Susannah Johnson gave birth to a baby girl, Elizabeth Captive Johnson, on August 31 in what is now Reading, Vermont, the site today marked by stones that Susannah had placed there in 1799. After having given birth, Johnson carried her newborn infant the rest of the trip.

Once in Canada, though, her husband was paroled so that he could return home to try and raise ransom money, Susannah Johnson and her children remained in captivity, part of the time spent in a criminal jail, the rest in a civil jail under better conditions, before finally being paroled in July 1757. She was finally reunited with her husband in Charlestown in January 1758, but was not reunited with her oldest son until October of that year, he having remained a captive with the Indians for all those years and barely remembering his mother. Susannah's happiness was short-lived, as her husband, James, was soon sent for military duty in Canada, where he was killed in action in July 1758.

Susannah subsequently lived in Charlestown, supported herself and her family by running a store, as well as being compensated by the New Hampshire Provincial government for the family's wartime losses. In 1762, the widow Johnson married John Hastings, and many years later in 1796 published an account of her time in captivity. Her excellent work, *A Narrative of the Captivity of Mrs. Johnson*, was widely read and went through several editions before her death in 1810. Among the most captivating passages in the book are those describing her childbirth while in captivity, and the subsequent close bond she retained with her daughter, Captive Johnson, through the remainder of her life.

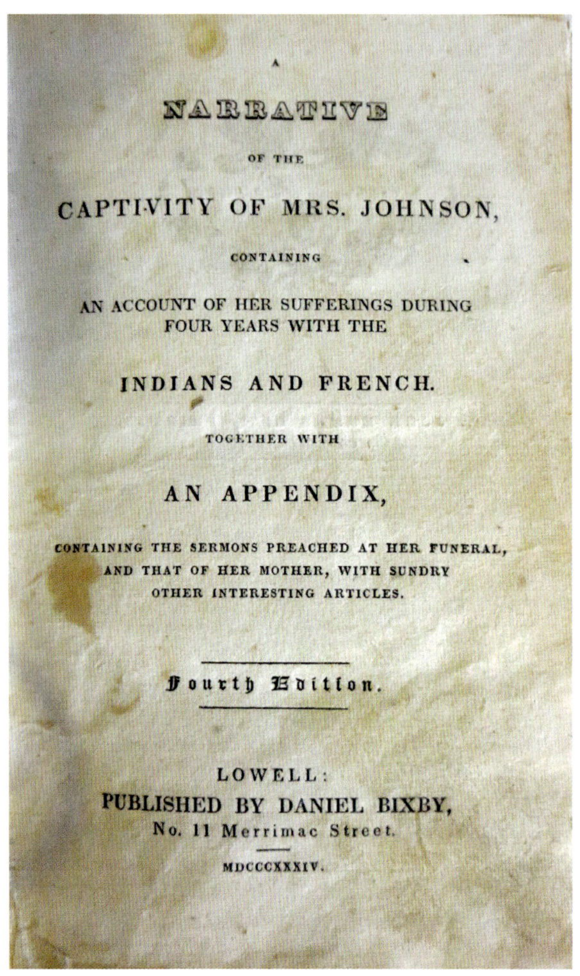

Title page of Susannah Johnson's captive narrative, fourth edition, 1834.

Johnson Family monument, Forest Hill Cemetery, Charlestown. This was erected in 1870 by the town and dedicated on the anniversary of the day Johnson was taken captive. Her small, plain gravestone dated 1810 is close-by.

Elizabeth "Molly" Page Stark (1737–1814), Stark Cemetery, Manchester

This esteemed woman, whose name, "Molly Stark," is well-known and has been given to many landmarks and locations in New England and beyond, is actually like most colonial-era women in that we know few details of her real life. Elizabeth Page was born in Haverhill, Massachusetts, the daughter of Elizabeth Merrill Page and Caleb Page, but when her mother died when she was just five years old, Elizabeth went to live with her widowed aunt, Ruth Wallingford, and would stay with her for ten years. In the meantime, her father, Captain Caleb Page, became a founder of Starkstown (later Dunbarton), and worked as a merchant and surveyor, employing his daughter's future husband, John Stark, during his road-building expedition to Coos in 1753.

Elizabeth Page married John Stark in 1758 and they would have a long life together, she bearing him eleven children, including their oldest son, Caleb, named after her father. Legend has it that John Stark had many names of endearment for his wife, "Molly" being perhaps the most common. While there are many stories about Molly Stark, it is hard to separate fact from fiction. While her husband gained fame as a fighter in both the French and Indian War and the American Revolution and was often away from home for long periods of time, Molly was left at home to care for her large family. Might she have shot a bear, as historical lore states, to protect her family? Did she, as a young girl, stand as a sentinel, looking out for Indians while her father and brothers were plowing the fields. Quite possibly both events are true, though there is no evidence that, contrary to legend, she ever fired a weapon during the American Revolution. There is also, in the Stark family lore, the story that states she served as a lookout on horseback for her husband while the British were evacuating Boston in March of 1776, but this has largely been disproven by historians.

So, why is Molly Stark so famous? Well, it is due to the words of her venerated husband, General John Stark (he who also coined that phrase, "Live free or die," that would become the New Hampshire state motto), during the Battle of Bennington on August 16, 1777, when he led a force of New Hampshire, Vermont, and Massachusetts militiamen against an invading force of German soldiers detached from British General John Burgoyne's army. Stark rallied his men at the start of the action with a battle cry which ended with the words "There are your enemies, the Red Coats and the Tories. They are ours, or this night Molly Stark sleeps a widow." With this stirring declaration and a large force of militia to back up his words, the battle was a decisive victory for Stark and the Americans, and made both him and his wife a legend. It was the type of battle cry that his men could easily get behind, one underscoring not liberty or the concept of a new country, but the more immediate concerns of protecting home and family.

Of course, had Stark and his men lost the battle, the remembrance of Molly Stark in legend would have not occurred and she might be little remembered today. I have to admit that I debated the inclusion of Molly Stark in this work, but after reading the words of New England humorist Judson Hale—he stating that "she never said or did anything of note. Nothing."—I changed my mind. What we do know is that she raised the Stark's eleven children, one of whom died young, that she supported her general-husband in every way that she could, to the point of inspiring a battle cry that resulted in an important victory, and when New Hampshire troops suffered an outbreak

Stark Family monument, Stark Park, Manchester. Note that the death date for Elizabeth Page Stark is incorrect, she dying in 1814, not 1794.

of smallpox, she helped nurse some of them back to health. That is not "nothing." Just as John Stark is venerated in New Hampshire for his words and deeds, so too does his wife deserve her place in history.

Molly Stark, who by all accounts was strong in both mind and body her entire life, contracted typhus fever in June of 1814 and succumbed to the disease five days later. Of the places and artifacts in New Hampshire that recall the memory of Molly Stark are the Molly Stark home in Dunbarton, where Elizabeth Page lived as a child, as well as the Molly Stark cannon in New Boston, an artillery piece captured by Stark's force at the Battle of Bennington and subsequently used by American forces before its capture in the War of 1812 and subsequent recapture from the British. Later on, it was presented by Stark to the Ninth Regiment of New Hampshire Militia and the New Boston Artillery Company (possibly around the time of Molly Stark's death) for the part they played in the Battle of Bennington and it is today the oldest cannon anywhere still in use.

Lucy Howe Crawford (1793-1869), Crawford Cemetery, Carroll

When we think of pioneer families in the White Mountains of New Hampshire, no family looms larger than that of the Crawfords. While Abel Crawford and his son, Ethan Allan Crawford, are the best-known members, perhaps, of this legendary family, their achievements would not have gained the high recognition they rightly deserve without the efforts of Lucy Howe Crawford, the wife of Ethan Allen. Indeed, it is through her book, *The History of the White Mountains*, first written in 1846, that we get a look at the region's early history.

Lucy Howe was born in Guildhall, Vermont, the daughter of Samuel and Mercy Rosebrook Howe, she being a cousin to Ethan Allen Crawford, they sharing the same grandparents, Eleazer and Hannah Rosebrook. Lucy and Ethan Allen knew one another growing up, but became close when she was sent for to care for Eleazer Rosebrook in Carroll, New Hampshire, during his final illness in 1817, while Ethan Allen was sent for to run the Rosebrook farm. Both Eleazer and his wife expressed the hope that Lucy and Ethan Allen might join together. This they did after Eleazer Rosebrook's death, Lucy marrying Ethan Allen Crawford in November 1817. The couple would subsequently make their home in the White Mountain wilderness, known for pioneering and catering to the early tourist trade for those who wanted to climb Mount Washington.

Lucy well knew, from the stories her grandmother Hannah told her, of the privations of living in the area. Indeed, Hannah Rosebrook first lived in a log cabin, arriving in Colebrook from Grafton, Massachusetts in 1773, and while her husband was out of the area, had to tend to the children and carried an infant child in her arms while searching for a lost cow! Lucy Howe Crawford, too, became a mother, bearing nine children in all, and suffering many setbacks, including the burning of the Crawford home. Most importantly, she was an excellent partner to her husband—while he was guiding tourists up the mountains, she ran their boarding house, tending to guests, sometimes in groups of fifty or more. Lucy, too, was an able hiker and climber; when one female guest insisted that she accompany their party to the top of Mount Washington, she did so, returning back down with hardly any assistance except in the location of Jacob's Ladder (where the Mt. Washington Cog Railway runs today).

Not only was Lucy Crawford a fierce protector of her husband's reputation, she "was always calm and unruffled," perhaps in contrast to her at times impetuous husband. She wrote her work not just as a record of the region and her family's history, but also as a way to raise funds after her husband's financial setbacks later in life. The year after her husband's death in 1846, Lucy Crawford left the White Mountains of New Hampshire to live the remainder of her life in more comfortable circumstances with her children in Lowell, Massachusetts. Upon her death, she was returned to New Hampshire to the place she called "My home! My home, my mountain home" to be buried.

Crawford Family monument, Crawford Cemetery, Carroll.

5

ARTS, EDUCATION, IDEALS, AND RELIGION

For such a small state, when it comes to this broad beliefs-based category, New Hampshire has what many might consider as surprising a fair number of candidates to choose from. No matter what field these women were working in, it was all about ideas and knowledge, and sharing it with a wider audience. Most of these women worked at the local level, and after their deaths, they have been largely forgotten.

TABITHA GILMAN TENNEY (1762–1837), WINTER STREET CEMETERY, EXETER

In this prominent Seacoast town, within an old burying ground, you will find a small, white, weather-worn monument. It does not stand out in anyway, except for the fact that someone in town keeps it decorated with flowers at varying times of the year, even when the surrounding gravestones here, many of them broken and shattered in pieces, lie forgotten and neglected. It was for this reason alone that I decided to take a look at Tabitha Tenney, a woman I had never heard of before. It turns out that, in her day, she was a bestselling author, probably one of the greatest bestselling female novelists in America from 1800 until Harriet Beecher Stowe published *Uncle Tom's Cabin* in 1852.

She was the daughter of Samuel and Lydia Gilman, a prominent family in Exeter, and while details of her education are unknown, her writing makes clear that she was well-read in all the classics. She was married in 1788 to Samuel Tenney of Newbury, Massachusetts, who had served in the American Revolution as a surgeon before coming to Exeter and taking up a career in politics, serving in the House of Representatives from 1800–1807. The couple would have no children. Considered quite the eligible bachelor, Tenney courted both Tabitha Gilman, a "practical, reserved, and somber" woman, and Martha "Patty" Rogers, the daughter of Reverend Daniel Rogers at the same time, Ms. Rogers calling Gilman "particularly disagreeable" in her personal diary for no stated reason.

Tenney wrote her first book in 1799, an instructional anthology, with her second book coming out in 1801. This book, a novel, was entitled *Female Quixotism: Exhibited in the Romantic Opinions and Extravagant Adventures of Dorcasina Sheldon* and, as

Tabitha Tenney, 1837, Winter Street Burial Ground, Exeter.

was typical of the time for women writers, was published anonymously. Following the adventures of a young woman, possibly based on Patty Rogers, who is seeking romantic adventure, Tenney's book, a parody of *Don Quixote*, is seen as a satirical work and a warning to mothers about their daughters to "Suffer not their imaginations to be filled with ideas of happiness, particularly in the connubial state, which can never be realized. Describe life to them as it really is." While this book fell out of popularity after 1846 and was out of print after the 1850s for over 100 years, it today is seen as an early work of feminism and thus historically important. Ironically, the book's satire was lost on many women and had the opposite intended effect of encouraging romanticism and the reading of "silly" books and Tenney later, without success, sought to stop future editions of the book from coming out. After the death of her husband in 1816, Tabitha Tenney, who wrote a third book (a cookbook) lived alone in their house on Front Street (now relocated to 65 High Street), dying in May 1837 after a brief illness. Forgotten after her death, Tenney today has been rediscovered by literary historians both locally and beyond, and her bestselling book has been the subject of countless scholarly articles and lectures.

CATHERINE FISKE (1784-1837), WASHINGTON STREET CEMETERY, KEENE

Unlike the modern era, educational opportunities for women in New Hampshire in the early days of our country were far from being equal with those for men. However, change would start to come when the Young Ladies Seminary was opened in Keene in 1814 by Miss Catherine Fiske. This distinguished educator was born in Worcester, Massachusetts, the daughter of Azubah Morse Fiske and Luther Fiske. Little is known of her early life, but most certainly she was destined to be an educator; by age fifteen, she was already a teacher working in Dover, Vermont.

Catherine Fiske would come to Keene by 1811, and three years later, in 1814, opened her own school, the Young Ladies Seminary, first aided by several other female teachers, including Miss Reed and Miss Elizabeth Sprague. Here, Fiske oversaw a curriculum for both girls and boys that included "all branches of learning," but also drawing, painting, and both "plain and ornamental needlework." The school was designed to improve young ladies' manners and morals and was considered one of the finest girl's schools in the entire country. Indeed, one of the first institutions of its kind for young girls in New England, Fiske's Young Ladies Seminary was a forerunner of the many female academies that were founded in New Hampshire and beyond in the 1820s and 1830s. In fact, young ladies from all over the country came to Fiske's school in Keene, she being considered "a remarkably efficient and successful teacher" who ran her school for most of its existence entirely on her own. In addition to her educational management, Fiske also oversaw the school's farm, its bread-making activities (done "on the scientific principles of chemistry"), and was said to do it all with "serenity and coolness."

At her death in 1837, the bells in town tolled, the stores closed, and "a long procession followed her to the grave." Her will left enough money to care for her mother, who died later in the same year, but also left a large contribution to the New Hampshire Asylum for the Insane. As for her school, it continued after her death for some ten years, but the Keene Academy (later Keene High School) drew pupils away, and with other teachers leaving, it eventually closed. It is hard to know just exactly how many lives Catherine Fiske's school enriched, but as the school's enrollment sometimes reached up to 100 students per term, estimates place the total number of female students at about 2,500 in all, a notable achievement for an extraordinary teacher.

FANNY SMITH (1780-1858), VILLAGE CEMETERY, PETERBOROUGH

Fanny Smith was the only daughter of William and Agnes Smith of Peterborough, the family being one of the most prominent in this Monadnock region town. Of Fanny's life, we know little: she never had children and lived a spinster her entire adult life, said to be eccentric. However, we also know that she was a woman with strongly-held beliefs who was not afraid to speak her mind. Because of her family's prominence, she had a high social standing in town, but used it to good effect, being a staunch advocate of the Abolitionist movement in the last decades of her life. Though uncertain, she may have been among those in town who invited Frederick Douglass to come to Peterborough in the 1840s to speak of his experiences as a slave.

Catherine Fiske, 1837, Washington
Cemetery, Keene.

Portrait of Catherine Fiske. (*Courtesy
Cheshire County Historical Society*)

Fanny, not surprisingly, held strong religious beliefs as well, her views being of the strict, Calvinist bent, and knew her religious doctrine well, the Peterborough town historian stating that "in her theological encounters with the ablest of her uncles, they did not always come off triumphant." Fanny Smith also put her religious tenets to work, walking the distance between Rindge and Peterborough every Sunday and teaching Sunday School classes in two different locales for some years. In short, as the town historian states, "Fanny was a woman of decided ability," and to the cause of abolition, she gave her all. In fact, her will dictated that funds from her estate were to go to promote the education of African American girls. The obelisk she caused to be erected memorialized her family on one side, and the cause of Abolition on another. Now faded by time and weather, it reads "this side of the column is devoted to the sacred cause of Emancipation. May God bless it, and all the people, say Amen!"

One cannot help but wonder what Fanny might have thought about old John Brown or Abraham Lincoln and the Civil War, but with her death in 1858, she would not bear witness to the painful events that eventually resulted in the freedom she so fervently hoped and prayed for.

MEHITABLE BEEDE WIGGIN (1800–1867), MASON CEMETERY, NORTH SANDWICH

The Beede family arrived early in Sandwich, with Jonathan and Anna Winslow Beede coming here from Fremont in 1784, living in a log cabin at the foot of Israel Mountain. The couple had many children, but of one of them, their daughter, Mehitable, we might not have much record were it not for the efforts of Carroll County historian Georgia Drew Merrill. In her book *History of Carroll County, New Hampshire*, published in 1889, she documents the lives of many prominent New Hampshire citizens in her genealogical sections for each town, but of these individuals, all are men save one, Mehitable Beede Wiggin. In her biography, Merrill states that "Mehitable early displayed a remarkable thirst for knowledge and a great desire to obtain a liberal education." We are lucky that she documented the life of this incredible woman, so I will let Merrill tell the rest of Wiggin's story:

Not content to stop with the mastery of the common English branches, she pushed her way into the realms of higher mathematics and the classics. After leaving the district school, she pursued her studies at Wolfeborough Academy, and at the Friend's School, Providence, R.I. At the later she was the first young lady who pursued the study of algebra. Passing from these schools she engaged in the study of languages under the direction of Rev. Samuel Hidden and her cousin, Aaron B. Hoyt. While studying with Mr. Hidden, she used to ride on horseback from her home to his house in Tamworth, a distance of ten miles, once a week, for the purpose of reciting to him. On these occasions it was no unusual thing for her to learn and recite double the lines of Virgil given her for a daily lesson. Indeed, her power of acquisition was remarkable. Before she was fifteen years of age she had learned and could recite the whole of Milton's Paradise Lost. She began teaching when sixteen years old, and continued to teach in public and private schools for half a century.... From childhood she took a deep

Above left: Smith Family monument, Village Cemetery, Peterborough.

Above right: Detail from Fanny Smith (1858) regarding the cause of Emancipation, Smith Family monument, Peterborough.

interest in the political events of the times, particularly in the great conflict over human slavery. Wherever human freedom was abridged or oppression existed, there her sympathies were enlisted … toward the poor her charity was boundless … as a ripe scholar, a successful teacher, and a Christian wife and mother, she had few equals in the community in which she lived.

A remarkable woman, indeed, and one that is eminently relatable today to all of those who can recall that special teacher in their life who helped and inspired them in some way, shape, or form. Mehitable Beede married Richard Wiggin in 1829 and would bear eight children, upon whom she worked her educational skills with the utmost dedication and care. So beloved was she in town, that when she died in 1867, she was "deeply mourned by a large circle of neighbors, pupils, and friends."

Mehitable Wiggin, 1867, Mason Cemetery, North Sandwich.

ABBY HUTCHINSON PATTON (1829–1892), NORTH YARD CEMETERY, MILFORD

If you have done any reading in nineteenth-century New Hampshire history, the name Abby Hutchinson is one you may have come across before. If you have not heard of her name specifically, the Hutchinson Family Singers may ring a bell—and well they should, for in the 1840s and 1850s, the members of this musical group were the most popular and influential entertainers in all of America. The Hutchinson Family Singers were from Milford, the children of Jesse and Mary Hutchinson. This couple had sixteen children in all, four of them daughters, of which thirteen lived to adulthood. The entire family got its start as a singing group in 1839 when they performed together in Milford, but four of them, John, Asa, Jesse, and Judson, formed a quartet in 1840 and began to give performances, at first in Milford and soon thereafter in Massachusetts.

Soon enough, in 1841, Jesse Hutchinson quit the group to become its manager and songwriter as their popularity grew, his place being taken by his sister, Abby Hutchinson, who was just twelve years old. With Abby singing as second tenor, the musical group would soon take the East Coast by storm, performing in New York City to rave reviews by 1843. The Hutchinson Family Singers are notable as being amongst the first popular music performers in America, they being so popular that they did a year-long tour in England in 1845, during which time they were entertained in the home of Charles Dickens and others in high society. While John Hutchinson was clearly the singing group's leader, Abby and the others all wrote songs for the group, their four-part harmony becoming a standard in American music for years after.

The group was also notable for the social causes, such as abolition, women's rights, and the temperance movement, which they supported and highlighted in their songs. Among the tunes penned by Abby Hutchinson was one she wrote about New Hampshire in 1850 called "Song of Our Mountain Home." Abby was known both for her sweet singing voice, a skill she inherited from her mother, and for her grace and charm, which she is said to have used to good effect to calm an unruly crowd when they were performing one of the group's abolitionist songs to a pro-slavery audience during one concert.

In February 1849, Abby Hutchinson married New York banker Ludlow Patton, subsequently giving up a full-time music career with her brothers at the insistence of her husband. However, she performed as a soloist over the years, particularly at women's suffrage events, and remained a crowd favorite, performing with her brothers on special occasions through the years, including their patriotic and freedom-related song concerts held in 1861 at the start of the Civil War. Abby Hutchinson Patton's influence was not only felt on the singing stage, but also in the press, she writing poems and other works in support of women's education and the suffrage movement in the years after the war.

Though the Patton's lived in New York and travelled extensively after Ludlow's retirement in 1873, Abby Hutchinson, who never had children of her own, always remained a New Hampshire woman at heart, spending many summers in her home state before being brought back to Milford after her death in 1892 for burial.

Abby Hutchinson Patton, 1892, North Yard Cemetery, Milford.

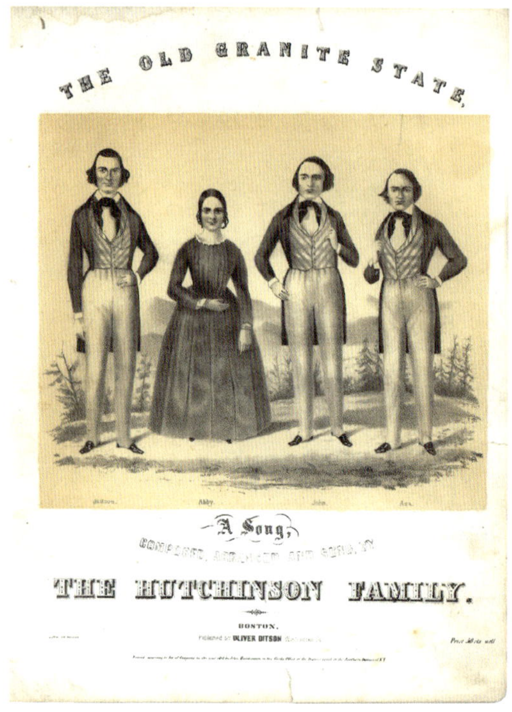

Sheet Music, "The Old Granite State",
Hutchinson Family Singers, 1843.

HANNAH ELIZABETH HALEY (1845-1897), TOWNHOUSE CEMETERY, TUFTONBORO

The daughter of Mary Neal Piper Haley and John Haley, Hannah was the youngest of three Haley children, and their only female child. From a young age, she was taught by her mother and likely attended the district school, but later would go to the distinguished Wolfeboro Academy. After her graduation there, she taught district school for a time, saving up enough money to go to college. She then attended Bates College in Lewiston, Maine, graduating in the class of 1873.

Haley preached her first sermon in Lowell, Massachusetts at the Free Chapel, whose minister was a relative, and afterwards attended divinity school at the Christian Biblical Institute in Stanfordville, New York. During her four years of study there, she gave sermons in the school chapel, as well as supplying the pulpits of neighboring towns on occasion. She was officially ordained as a minister on May 10, 1877, and for the following twenty years served as an evangelist preacher in many locales, including as far west as Ohio. She preached for a wide variety of church denominations, including Congregationalist, Methodist, Free Will Baptists, and Calvinistic Baptist, and was said to have inspired many religious conversions. She was not the first or only minister in the Haley family, for her older brother John Haley, who referred to her in his Tuftonboro town history as H. Lizzie Haley, was also a minister. However, she is important as being among the first group of women to be ordained in America, and was very likely the first New Hampshire woman to be ordained in an organized religion.

Rev. Hannah Elizabeth Haley, 1897, Town House Cemetery, Tuftonboro.

Sadly, her life was cut short when she died from liver disease in Lowell, Massachusetts. The Biblical inscription at the bottom of her stone, probably chosen by Haley's minister brother, epitomizes the work and legacy of Hannah Elizabeth Haley: "They that turn many to righteousness, shall shine as the stars, forever and ever."

AUGUSTA HARVEY WORTHEN (1821–1910), NORTH SUTTON CEMETERY, NORTH SUTTON

For most of the Granite State's history, at least when it comes to published works, the documenting of New Hampshire towns was a man's domain. That situation, however, would start to change in 1890 when Augusta Harvey Worthen published her exhaustive history of the town of Sutton, the first woman in the state ever to do so. While she was a ground-breaker in history, it really should come as no surprise, for she was already an accomplished educator and writer by then.

Augusta Harvey was born in Sutton, the daughter of Sally Greeley Harvey and John Harvey, prominent citizens in their town. At the age of eight, she was sent to live with her uncle, New Hampshire Governor Matthew Harvey, in Hopkinton for six years, attending the Hopkinton Academy. In 1839, at the age of sixteen, Augusta became a district teacher in Sutton before moving to Lowell, Massachusetts two years later. Here, she worked in the textile mills along with many other young women, attending school at night. During the three years she worked in the mills, Harvey wrote for the mill magazine, and attended Andover Academy, working off her tuition by serving as a teacher to some of the academy's younger students.

In 1855, Augusta Harvey married New Hampshire native Charles Worthen and lived with him first in Danvers, and then by 1858 in Lynn, Massachusetts, where he owned a shoe manufacturing business. Though she would live here the reminder of her life, Augusta Worthen never forgot her hometown and returned to Sutton often. After her marriage, she continued her literary writings and her poems were featured in several anthologies including *New Hampshire Poets*, *Poets of America*, and *Poets of Essex County*.

However, it is her town history of Sutton for which she is best remembered, she compiling the work over the course of twenty years beginning in 1870. Her diligence in collecting information about the town is clearly evident in her two-volume work, which is one of the best of New Hampshire's town histories in terms of accuracy and thoroughness, as well as readability. Her work in this area paved the way for subsequent female history writers, including Harriette Noyes in Hampstead.

Upon her death in 1910, it was said of Augusta Harvey Worthen that she "was possessed of strong mental endowments and marked literary ability" by the editors of the *Granite State Monthly* magazine.

Above: Augusta Harvey, 1910, North Sutton Cemetery, Sutton. Note the inscription "Historian of Sutton" at bottom right.

Right: Photo, Augusta Worthen, from A Woman of the Century (1893).

6

EXTRAORDINARY WOMEN LEADING EVERYDAY LIVES

The women highlighted here have several things in common. They are not famous in any way, and though some were well-known in their town in their own day, most of them lived what might be considered, for the day, normal, everyday, perhaps even invisible, lives. Second, most were hard-working women who did what they had to do to survive. For some, life was much easier than for others, but all of them stand out for such characteristics as an extraordinary work ethic and determination in the face of great odds. For these reasons, these women, despite the distance in time between their lives and ours, are eminently relatable, akin in many ways to the women in our lives who inspire us today.

BETSY PETTENGILL EASTMAN (1763–1867), SOUTH ROAD CEMETERY, SALISBURY

But for one moment in time, and one momentous event, perhaps nothing of Betsy Pettengill Eastman's life would be known. Betsy Pettengill was the daughter of Betty Heath Pettengill and Captain David Pettengill, the third oldest of their eleven children. Her parents were married in Salisbury, Massachusetts, and lived there prior to moving to Salisbury, New Hampshire, sometime between 1760 and 1767.

It may be that while the family was in the process of moving northward that Betsy stayed with her aunt and uncle, for on June 14, 1768, at the age of five, Betsy was travelling with her uncle Benjamin Pettengill to Salisbury, New Hampshire, stopping along the way at the house of family friends in South Hampton. While playing in a barn with her friends during this brief stopover, Betsy and her friends found a loose floorboard, and, upon lifting it up, found the body of a lifeless infant child. It would soon be discovered that the child was the newborn baby, having been born just four days before, of Miss Ruth Blay (born 1737 in Haverhill, Massachusetts), an unmarried schoolteacher who was living in town.

Soon enough, Ruth Blay would be taken into custody, charged with the capital crime of concealing the death of her illegitimate child. Despite the fact that the child was stillborn and did not die violently at the hands of her mother, Ruth Blay would eventually be hanged for her "crime," going to the gallows in Portsmouth in December 1768. Her trial was one that was heavily publicized and shook the New Hampshire colony to its core. Blay, as it turns out, would be the last woman to be executed in New Hampshire history.

For Betsy Pettengill, life went on, her role of discovery soon overshadowed by the events of the trial and execution. And yet, it was later said that the event "cast a gloom" over the rest of her life. It is interesting that Betsy's sister, Ruth Pettengill, was born four years later in 1772—did her mother choose this name with Ruth Blay in mind? Whatever the case may have been, Betsy went on with her life, moving with her parents to Salisbury, here marrying Joel Eastman in April 1785 and living on the farm presented to her by her father.

Betsy Pettengill Eastman would give birth to seventeen children, two of whom died in infancy, while her namesake daughter Betsey died at the age of fifteen. According to the Salisbury town history, Betsy Pettengill Eastman was known for "casting sunshine all around by her loveliness of disposition and genial temper," as well as "Her native wit." However, not all was sunshine for Betsy, for she often thought of Ruth Blay's trial and execution, "dwelling upon it with much sadness, and exhibiting great feeling and a spirit of compassion for the unfortunate victim, whose shameful death made a deep and lasting impression upon the public mind at the time."

In fact, Betsy "always had a lurking suspicion that Miss Blay was wrongfully executed" and "felt shocked at having contributed to the death of one who might have been "more sinned against than sinning." Was it perhaps because of her shocking discovery and subsequent doubts that Betsy would not "profess her faith in Jesus Christ" until December 1794 at the relatively late age of thirty-one? In the end, Betsy Pettengill Eastman led a long life and would subsequently be remembered for the fact that "No person ever left her door hungry, and among the poor she was particularly charitable."

Betsy Eastman, 1867, South Road Cemetery, Salisbury.

ESTHER WHIPPLE MULLINAUX (1784–1868), NORTH CEMETERY, PORTSMOUTH

Esther Whipple was born in Portsmouth, the oldest child of Dinah Chase Whipple and Prince Whipple, both of whom had once been enslaved. Her father, as well as her uncle, Cuffee Whipple, were forcibly enslaved and brought to this country against their will, while her mother was born into slavery, owned by Rev. Stephen Chase of neighboring New Castle. She was manumitted in 1781 at the age of twenty-one and soon after married Prince Whipple, who was owned by General William Whipple, a signer of the Declaration of Independence for New Hampshire and a former slave-trader.

Prince served prominently during the American Revolution as a kind of *aide-de-camp* to General Whipple, but also was one of twenty Portsmouth slaves who petitioned the New Hampshire legislature asking for their freedom in November 1779. However, he would only gain his freedom in February 1784 after his military service was over. Prince and Dinah Whipple were well-respected in Portsmouth's black community, as well as in the community at large, but life was still very difficult for free Blacks.

Esther married Portsmouth sailor William Mullinaux in April 1801, the couple having two children, William Prince and Anna. When her husband failed to return from a voyage and was presumed lost at sea, Esther remarried in 1815. However, the fact that she did not legally terminate her marriage did not sit well with North Church officials, where she was a devout member, and they publicly admonished her in 1817, she being required to read a confession of her sin to the assembled church body.

After the death of her second husband in 1827, Esther would marry for a third time, bearing three more children. Esther lived for much of her life with her mother, Dinah, who was widowed when Prince Whipple died in 1796, in the family home. After Dinah's death in 1846, Esther had to find a place of her own, living in a small house she rented and earning a living as a laundress. By 1851, Esther had worked hard enough to buy her own home on Walden Lane, where she lived the remainder of her years.

For her entire life, Esther was a devout worshiper at North Church in Portsmouth, and when she died, she left everything in her will to the church. She was buried in North Cemetery in a plot not far from her father. With the death of this good and godly woman, one of the last direct connections to the legendary Prince Whipple and the practice of slavery in Portsmouth was now no more. Marked burial sites for New Hampshire's earliest free-born African American citizens, many of whom lived in dire economic circumstances, are relatively few in number, so Esther Whipple Mullineaux's weather-worn gravestone is an important artifact in more than one way. It not only marks her final resting place, but also serves as a reminder of the evolution of race relations in New Hampshire from colonial times to the end of the Civil War.

MARGARET DAVIS (1797–1869), VILLAGE CEMETERY, JACKSON

When discussing the industries of the North Country of New Hampshire, most often one is inclined to think of the timber and lumber business. However, other smaller industries, cottage industries if you will, abounded. Perhaps none was more renowned in the early days before the Industrial Revolution in the town of Shelburne than the business conducted by Margaret "Peggy" Davis.

Above: Esther Mullineaux, 1868, North Cemetery, Portsmouth.

Right: Photo of Esther Mullineaux. (*Courtesy of The African American Resource Center, Portsmouth*)

I have been unable to discover much about the early life of Davis, other than the fact that she was likely born in Buxton, Maine, to Sylvanus and Hannah Gorham Davis (though her name is omitted from most Davis family genealogies) and was likely the older sister of Lot Davis, though she was usually referred to as "Aunt Peggy" around town. The *History of Coos County, New Hampshire* (1888), from which our entire knowledge of Davis is gathered, indicates that Margaret became blind at the age of 12 in 1809, but whether through accident or the onset of a medical condition is unknown. Her later family circumstances and how she came to live with Lot Davis are also unknown. However, it is written that "Her education was necessarily limited. Schools for the deaf, dumb, and blind were not for her", but that "She had learned to read and write, and to "work" letters on course canvas".

Margaret's mother, Hannah, died in 1807, so it is likely that not only had she taught Margaret some vital skills, but so too, perhaps, might her step-mother, Phebe McDonald Davis, have continued to do so while caring for her when she became blind. While Davis would always live with family members, she still found her own way and "became celebrated for her skill in sewing, spinning, and knitting," famed locally for the mittens and socks she crafted. She could not only "knit the alphabet," but could also "knit a verse," doing so on a pair of mittens for a man in town who had bet a friend that "there is not a woman in the state of New Hampshire" who could match her skill. Having heard of this bet, Margaret Davis, worked late into the night for several evenings creating a pair of mittens with four lines of verse about money and friendship, copies of these same mittens subsequently requested by family and friends. Whether or not any of these mittens have survived in the area as treasured family heirlooms is unknown, but I hope so.

Margaret Davis would later live in Gorham, New Hampshire, after Lot Davis moved there in the 1830s, and belonged to the Free Will Baptist Church. It is said that Gorham, New Hampshire, was named after Hannah Gorham Davis, the mother of Margaret and Lot Davis, at the suggestion of Lot Davis. Margaret Davis would spend the last years of her life living in Jackson in the household of her niece, Almeda Davis Dearborn, and was buried in the Dearborn family plot in the Village Cemetery upon her death.

MARY CAMPBELL (1784-1873), SALEM CENTER BURYING GROUND, SALEM

The subject of this sketch, in reality, defies categorization, but one thing we do know is this: Mary Campbell was certainly an interesting woman. Everything we know of her comes from Salem author and town historian Edgar Gilbert. Mary was the daughter of Elizabeth and Robert Campbell, her father a man of means who served at some time as a district schoolteacher. His daughter, possibly the couple's only child, never married, but supported herself in a variety of ways. She was a schoolteacher, possibly her first occupation, but also owned a shoe shop, working as a cobbler making and repairing shoes. Yet another of her occupations was that of keeper of the tolls at the Canobie Lake Station on the Londonderry Turnpike Road which ran from the Massachusetts state line to Concord. As far as other details about Mary Campbell, Gilbert has this to say in his *History of Salem*:

> She was a very tall, angular woman, with muscles like a man, developed by the active life
> she led. She kept a gun in her house, with which she was said to be very proficient. In the
> wide forests that then surrounded her habitation many a partridge fell beneath her unerring

Above left: Margaret Davis, 1869, Village Cemetery, Jackson.

Above right: Mary Campbell, 1873, Salem Center Burying Ground, Salem.

aim. But she was not dependent entirely upon her own efforts for her supply of game. The large cat that shared her board was so well trained that he contributed largely to the fare.

And that is the sum of what is known of Mary Campbell; it is not much, but it is enough to make her worthy of inclusion as a true woman of granite.

SARAH JOY GRIFFITHS (1821–1887), JOY FAMILY CEMETERY, DURHAM

The Joy Family Cemetery in Durham, located on Packers Falls Road, has been the subject of curiosity, for over 100 years now. The story centers on a family dispute about a monument placed here for Sarah Griffiths in 1887, and the "spite stone" subsequently erected by her brother, Samuel Joy. It is a story that pits a seemingly greedy or politically motivated brother against a sister who was honoring the last will and testament of another sister, resulting in legal proceedings that made it all the way to the New Hampshire Supreme Court. However, much of the telling of this story over the years has revolved around Samuel Joy and his actions, while his recently deceased sister is largely an afterthought. Sarah Joy was the third child of Nancy Watson Joy and Ebenezer Joy.

Her early life details are unknown, but as a young woman she made her way to Manchester, possibly one of the hundreds of girls from rural communities to seek employment in the mills there. Many of these young women would work in the mills for a few years before getting married and settling down to have a family. That is what Sarah Joy may have done, for on February 1, 1846, she was married in Manchester to David Griffiths of Durham and would move back to her hometown.

The couple would have one child, Martha Frances, who was born in 1847 but died two years later in September 1849. The Joy family farm was deeded to David Griffiths, but after his untimely death in 1855, Sarah Joy Griffiths was its owner before selling it to a family member in 1866. The remainder of Sarah Griffiths' life details are a bit obscure as to where she lived and how she may have supported herself. She later lived in Manchester on Chestnut Street, where she died from liver cancer in 1887.

That is where the legends start, for in her will, she specified that from her sizeable estate of $10,000, part of it was to be used to "erect a suitable monument, and fit up the lot," by which she meant that the Joy Family Cemetery would have the stone fence surrounding it repaired or replaced. The rest of the money was divided between her older sister, Nancy Joy Fesler, and her brother, Samuel Joy. As for the family cemetery, the funds left for its upkeep were the first such private cemetery trust ever accepted by the town. Nancy Fesler took matters into her own hands as executor and intended to erect a large granite monument to mark the graves of Sarah Joy Griffiths, as well as those of her husband David and infant daughter Martha, at a cost of about $3,500 (accounts vary).

This should have been the end of the story, right? It was not; Samuel Joy disputed the expense for such a large monument, taking legal action, which he lost after it went to the state's highest court, thus ending several years of litigation. Shortly thereafter, the Griffiths monument was erected and the stone wall around the family cemetery fitted up. It is said in town lore that Samuel at one point had placed a board fence near Sarah's grave with the words "A $3,000 grave" painted on it. When this was removed by Sarah's husband's nephews, Samuel Joy subsequently carved a "spite stone," which was placed a short distance away and featured a hand pointing toward the Griffith's gravesite with the words "A suitable monument and fit up the lot," followed by Sarah's initials. As if this was not strange enough, he carved the words "I am a socialist" on the central monument in the Joy Family Cemetery on the side bearing his name.

Both of these stones survive and are what drive people to the cemetery today. It is hard to tell what Samuel Joy's problem was. Did he feel that his inheritance might have been bigger if the money had not been spent on a big monument? Or, most likely, was he offended by what he saw as an outrageous expense for a monument based on his political views? Interestingly, a chapter of the Socialist Party was formed in neighboring Dover, composed mainly of area farmers like Samuel Joy, beginning in 1893 due to heavy interest.

No matter what his problem was, the unsung hero in this episode is Nancy Joy Fesler, who respected her younger sister's wishes and saw that they were carried out in the face of bullying tactics by an unhappy brother. Today, the sister's lie side by side, Nancy Fesler choosing to be buried here after her death in Lowell, Massachusetts, in 1894, the bonds of sisterhood remaining unbroken.

Right: Sarah Griffiths monument, 1887, Joy Family Cemetery, Durham.

Below: Joy Family Cemetery, Durham. In front is the "spite stone" erected by Samuel Joy, with a hand pointing towards his sister's monument at left, the words on the stone from Sarah Griffiths' will.

SAMANTHA PLANTIN (1827-1899), DORCAS BREWER PLANTIN (1780-1872), AND MAHALA PLANTIN (1805-1837), VALLEY STREET CEMETERY, MANCHESTER

Few African Americans were living in the big city of Manchester when Samantha Plantin made her way here from her home in neighboring New Boston. While we know little about her family background, what few details we have of her own life demonstrates that she was a hard-working woman of the highest character. Also buried here in Valley Street Cemetery next to Samantha are two other black women, Mahala Plantin, whose relationship to Samantha is uncertain, and Dorcas Brewer Plantin, who was likely her grandmother, and possibly the daughter of Revolutionary War soldier Peter Brewer who was killed in the Battle of Saratoga. Both women died and were buried in New Boston, but were later reburied here. Dorcas Brewer, who married Paoli Plantin in Weare on April 28, 1818, lived in their house on Weare Road, across from Dodge Pond (once called "N****r" Pond due to their proximity) and worked right up to the end of her life in New Boston, employed as a housekeeper as late as 1870, a path that her grand-daughter would follow, almost certainly due to economic necessity.

Life was not easy in this time for a young, single woman on her own, and was even more difficult for a black woman. Samantha left her home in New Boston about 1847, coming to Manchester to find employment. According to the New Boston Historical Society, she was employed as a washerwoman and a dress-maker, and by 1880, if not sooner, was working in one of the textile mills. Almost from the time of her arrival in town, she was a member of the Merrimack Street Baptist Church, being a devout and esteemed member of their congregation for over five decades.

By 1890, Samantha had saved up enough wages to have a house of her own built on Concord Street. It was some years later, in 1895, that she also had her family burials relocated here from New Boston. Though she never married, it was said that Samantha had many friends, who helped her in her final days before she died from pneumonia. Upon her death, with no surviving members, she left some of the proceeds of her estate to local charities in Manchester, but the greatest amounts went to the Tuskegee Institute in Alabama and the Haines Normal and Industrial Institute in Augusta, Georgia, well-known African American schools.

LUCY DEANE JACKSON BLAKE (1834-1927), ORDINATION ROCK CEMETERY, TAMWORTH

I first "met" Lucy Blake through the efforts of Tamworth historical role-player and library staff member Peggy Johnson in 2019 while leading a tour and joint presentation through Ordination Rock Cemetery. I knew straight away that Lucy was a woman who was worthy of inclusion in this work. Not only did she lead a long and productive, and hard life, but she left the letters and diaries—her own words—to document it. Lucy Jackson was born in Tamworth to Elizabeth and Charles Jackson, and by the time of her marriage to Ira Blake in May 1860, she was employed as a schoolteacher. Their son, Henry, was born the following year, in 1861, and later that year, Lucy's husband enlisted for service in the Civil War, joining the Second Regiment of U.S. Sharpshooters in December.

Samantha Plantin, 1899,
Valley Street Cemetery,
Manchester.

Portrait photo of Samantha Plantin,
c. 1860s. (*Courtesy of the New
Boston Historical Society*)

It was a trying time for Lucy, left with an infant son and a husband heading off to war, she writing in her diary on December 9, 1861: "This has been a trying day for me. My Dear Husband has enlisted in the United States Service…. What shall I do I must do as well as I can." Two days later, with Ira Blake headed off to war, she wrote "Ira has gone. I am very much afraid I shall never see him again." In the days, weeks, and months to follow, Lucy records many of her day-to-day activities in her diary, as well as her thoughts and feelings. She talks about her loneliness and the difficulties enduring the winter weather, as well as her premonitions about her husband. On April 7, 1862, she writes: "I am very low spirited today. I do not know why I should be. I feel just as though Ira was in battle today or as though I was going to hear some thing bad in regard to him." These are thoughts that any military spouse can understand even to this day.

The following year, on her birthday in April, she wrote: "This is my birthday. I am 29 years old today. I have been dropping corn today, got very tired. I am glad it is done … I am in hopes that Ira will be home as soon as next spring." Indeed, Ira Blake did come home, but only for a month before he headed back off to war. On June 24, 1864, Lucy received word that her husband had been wounded in the left leg. She writes: "I must wait with patience till I hear he is in the hands of a just God. He will do all things right and well." However, Lucy decided not to wait, and started off in a coach from Tamworth to make her way to see Ira in the military hospital at Alexandria, Virginia, departing on July 20, 1864 and arriving days later. She would spend several months with Ira while he was in the hospital, sitting with him twelve hours a day. At first, things looked promising, she writing that "I found Ira better than I expected", but soon enough her husband started to fail, "losing strength every day."

She was beside his bed on the day he died, October 27, 1864, writing: "He was so pressed for breath, he suffered very much still 12 o'clock he breathed his last what a sad day. I have lost one of the best of Husbands … I am left alone here now." Lucy began her sad journey home the day after Ira Blake died, arriving in Tamworth on November 2. The following day, she paid a visit to Ordination Rock Cemetery "to look out a place to bury Ira," and now had to wait for his body to be returned home, she being "most sick, my back is so lame I can barely move." Ira's body arrived home on November 5, 1864, and he was buried on November 9, Lucy writing: "they have laid my darling Ira in his grave. I cannot hardly realize it."

It would take years for Lucy to overcome this loss, and perhaps she never did emotionally. On the tenth anniversary of her husband's death in 1874, she wrote in her diary: "I am so lonesome I do not know what to do with myself." But, in reality, she did know what to do with herself. Despite the fact that she never remarried, Lucy Blake supported herself and her son by teaching school again, keeping lodgers, as well as maintaining her farm and selling its products, and even worked as a washer-woman. She did what she had to do to survive, and did it largely by herself, a granite woman if ever there was one.

Lucy Blake, 1927, Ordination Rock Cemetery, Tamworth.

Portrait photo of Lucy Blake, *c.* 1861. (*Courtesy of the Cook Memorial Library, Tamworth*)

7

WOMEN OF MEDICINE

In our nation's history, we have always struggled with gender equality when it comes to the field of medicine, and that struggle continues to this day, even though it has been proven that a gender-balance in medicine improves health outcomes for all patients. Of course, in New Hampshire and beyond, women have always had traditional roles as caregivers and caretakers, whether it be in the home raising and caring for their sick children, or outside the home as midwives and, later on, as nurses. However, the careers of the outstanding women below show not only how New Hampshire women excelled in these roles, but are also indicative of the progress and advances that were made over the years. More success would follow in the twentieth century, but these women helped pave the way.

FREELOVE BUELL NETTLETON (1737–1825), PINE STREET EAST CEMETERY, NEWPORT, AND MABEL NETTLETON BUELL (1762–1851), MAPLE STREET CEMETERY, NEWPORT

The unsung medical heroes in the early history of any New Hampshire town were those women that were midwives and, in many cases, *de facto* doctors, helping to deliver babies and give medical aid and advice long before the first trained doctors arrived in town. Sadly, in many towns these names have been lost to history, but not so for the town of Newport, where the medical skills of two women, a mother and daughter duo, were celebrated for decades after their deaths.

Freelove Buell, who went by the name of "Love," was from Killingworth, Connecticut, where she married Jeremiah Nettleton in November 1760. Soon thereafter, in 1762, the first of their six children, Mabel Nettleton, was born. The family moved to Newport in 1779, among a later wave of settlers to arrive here from Killingworth after the town was first settled in 1763. While Jeremiah Nettleton was a large land owner and a respected citizen, it was Love Nettleton who was an even greater asset to her new community. While there were certainly midwives in Newport before Love Nettleton, it is her name that is the earliest remembered and whose renown spread even beyond the town borders.

The historian of Newport, when discussing the town's medical history, recalls that she "possessed unusual skill as a midwife" and was diligent in carrying out her duties no matter what the conditions. It was recalled in 1846, many years after the event, that in 1780 Love Nettleton walked three miles in snowshoes "to discharge her duties," and that on one occasion her skills were required in neighboring New London, she being drawn there on a hand-sled by four men. Those were the days, indeed, when house calls were the norm, but it is clear that Love Nettleton was no ordinary midwife.

Perhaps not surprisingly, she passed these skills on to her daughter, Mabel, who we can imagine by her early teens was accompanying her mother on her medical calls and learning all the while. Though we know less about Mabel Nettleton's specific actions, it is significant to note that one nineteenth-century historian called her, at the age of twenty-eight or less, the "only physician" in Newport for several years, before the arrival of Dr. James Corbin in 1790. That one line tells us all we need to know about Mabel's skills in the medical arts. Though details are unknown, Mabel, who married Aaron Buell, Jr., and came to be called "Aunt Mabel," continued in her medical field, certainly as a midwife, and perhaps as a physician when the town's only trained doctor was unavailable. Freelove Nettleton's weather-worn gravestone (not pictured), can be found at the rear of the Pine Street East Cemetery.

Mabel Buell, 1852, Maple Street Cemetery, Newport.

LUCINDA S. CAPEN, M.D. (1815-1890), MILLVILLE CEMETERY, CONCORD

Can someone tell me, please, why there is, as of this writing, no State Historical Marker in Concord for a woman who was not only the state's first female doctor, but the first woman ever to graduate with a medical degree from a New England medical college? Though Capen's career was documented early on in The New England Journal of Medicine (1934), she has still received far too little publicity. Capen was born in Stewartstown, the fifth child of Anna Carter Capen and Ebenezer Capen, and moved to Concord with the family about 1825 and would marry Robert Hall, in 1833. Her husband developed an interest in herbal medicine and began working with Dr. Lemuel Paige in Weare and became an apothecary (pharmacist). He would soon manufacture and sell his own herbal remedies.

Lucinda Hall also became interested in medicine and worked with Dr. Paige, but with an eye towards becoming a doctor. Because no medical schools at that time, and for many years after, admitted women, she attended the newly-formed Boston Female Medical College to study midwifery and, in 1850, was in their first graduating class, returning to Concord to become the first women in the state to hold a medical certificate of any kind. Still desirous of gaining a doctor's degree, Capen enrolled in the Worcester Medical College in Massachusetts in 1852, and was in their first class of graduates, thereby becoming the first woman to graduate from a medical college in New England. It is interesting to note that not only was Dr. Capen (who practiced under her maiden name) the first such graduate in New England, but the first in her family to graduate

Hall Family monument, Lucinda Capen Hall (1890), Millville Cemetery, Concord.

with a medical degree—her husband, Dr. Robert Hall, would graduate with a medical degree at the same college two years later.

The couple would later set up a practice in Lowell, Massachusetts, and though little is known about their practice there, it is highly likely that their patients included the mill workers in that town, many of whom were women. With the accidental death of the couple's son in 1856 and the early death of a married daughter in 1857, the Halls returned to Concord, where they would practice the remainder of their life. In 1867, they opened a fifty-bed sanitarium/health resort next to their home, which remained in operation until it burned down in 1885. Dr. Lucinda Capen retired from practice in 1876 due to poor health, though she still treated former patients and friends from time to time. She died in 1890 from apoplexy and the effects of bronchitis, and it is interesting to note that her death record lists her occupation as that of "housewife." However, her husband made sure that her accomplishments were noted on the Hall family monument in the Millville Cemetery, a public declaration of an achievement that is otherwise hidden in plain sight.

Harriet Patience Dame (1815–1900), Blossom Hill Cemetery, Concord

When the history of the Second Regiment of New Hampshire Volunteers was written in full by former soldier Martin Haynes in 1896, he had this to say of Harriet Dame and her service in the Civil War:

> [She was] one of the genuine heroines of the war…. It is a name that will not be found on any official roster of the Second Regiment; but she was with them, she was of them, and was and is honored and respected and loved by her old comrades with a depth of affection that can find no adequate expression in words.

Indeed, if ever a woman was a "Granite" woman, it was Dame, and her service in the Civil War proves it over and over again. Dame was the daughter of Phebe and James Dame of Barnstead; little is known of her early life, but she would eventually make her way to Concord, where in 1860, on the eve of the Civil War, she was working as a boarding-house keeper. Dame was not married by this time, and remained single her entire life.

When in May 1861, after the Civil War began, state regiments began mustering in and around Concord, she opened her home for any of the new recruits that were sick, and in June 1861, when the Second Regiment headed south to the war effort, she joined them as a hospital matron. While she had an offer to join a surgical unit elsewhere, she decided to stay with the boys she knew, and followed the orders of regimental commander Col. Gilman Marston, who told her not to "desert" the regiment. She would subsequently serve as a regimental and corps nurse, even though she had no prior training, for the next four years and endured the same hardships that the New Hampshire soldiers did. Marston would later say of Dame: "Wherever the regiment went she went, often going on foot, and sometimes camping on the field without a tent…. She was truly an angel of mercy, the bravest woman I ever knew. I have seen her face a battery without flinching."

Indeed, Dame did not just serve in a hospital setting; when the regiment had to make a sudden retreat during the Seven Days' Battles campaign, the men in the hospital left behind and facing certain capture, Dame stayed with them and led them on a march for safety at Harrison's Landing, bringing every man but one to safety. During the Battle of Fair Oaks in June 1862, she spent the night in the trenches with the soldiers, caring for all the wounded, not just the men in her own regiment, the only nurse present. Later that month, while caring for the wounded during the Battle of Oak Grove, she was tending to the wounded when she discovered that of the several men killed in the battle from the regiment, one of them was a neighbor boy whom she had known since childhood. She subsequently prepared his body, along with others, for burial and "saw them laid in the ground at the foot of an oak tree near the hospital." In fact, Dame often went above and beyond her normal duties, she also writing letters home for the men.

In July 1862, she was captured during the Battle of Malvern Hill by an enemy picket, but was able to escape on her own. In August 1862, while stationed at the hospital in Centreville during the Second Battle of Bull Run, she was captured for a second time and sent to the tent of none other than Confederate General Thomas "Stonewall" Jackson, but was soon released and sent back to the Union lines when she showed him the bandages and medicines she was carrying. Interestingly, she was often accompanied during her hospital duties by her two dogs, Whisky and Quinine, surely favorites of her "boys," too. In July 1863, she was with the regiment at Gettysburg, where she tended to the Union Army's heavy casualties and in the winter of 1863, she was in charge of relief efforts for New Hampshire soldiers in Washington, D.C.

The following spring in 1864, Dame took on an even bigger role when she was appointed matron for the Army's XVIII Corps hospital, in charge of all nurses, during the campaign to capture Richmond. Dame was not only in charge of large-scale nursing efforts, but now took on additional supply and inspection duties. At the end of the war, Dame stayed in Washington, D.C., where she was offered a clerk position in the Treasury Department in 1867, and later served as the third president of the National Association of Army Nurses of the Civil War, a group which advocated for army nurses, seeking benefits and recognition for their service.

In 1884, Dame received a government pension for her service after over 600 soldiers, men who appreciated her services like none other, signed a petition to the Senate. Though she lived away from her home state for many years until returning home shortly before her death in 1900, she never forgot New Hampshire and the men she served with. She regularly attended the annual Civil War encampment reunions held at the Weirs every summer, and donated the funds for the building of the Second Regiment headquarters at the encampment site in 1886. During her military service, Dame earned many honors, including a gold badge from the Second New Hampshire Regiment, as well as medals from three of the corps she served with. Most notable is the prominent granite monument which marks her final resting place—it is topped off with the diamond insignia of the III Corps of the Army of the Potomac, in which she served from 1862–1864.

In 1901, the year after her death, Harriet Dame's portrait was hung in the New Hampshire State House, the first woman in the state to be so honored, and a most fitting public tribute to a compassionate and brave woman. That same year, the annual Civil War Encampment at the Weirs was also named in her honor. Just over 100 years later, in 2002, Harriet Dame received further recognition when she was inducted into the American Nurses Association Nursing Hall of Fame.

Above left: Harriet Dame, 1900, Blossom Hill Cemetery, Concord.

Above right: Portrait painting of Harriet Dame (1901), which hangs in the New Hampshire Statehouse. Note the medals for her service.

Right: Detail, Harriet Dame monument. The diamond at top was the emblem of the Third Corps, Army of the Potomac.

ESTHER HILL HAWKS, M.D. (1833–1906), PINE GROVE CEMETERY, MANCHESTER

Esther Hill Hawks simple monument says it all: "Army Nurse, ASST. Surgeon, Teacher of Freedmen, Physician." This native daughter, as her epitaph implies, led an incredible life, and has even had a portion of her diaries published, yet remains but little remembered in New Hampshire.

Esther Hill was born in Hooksett, the daughter of Jane Kimball Hill and Parmenas Hill, one of eight children. She went to public school in several different towns, and attended high school in Manchester. Afterwards, she attended Kingston Academy, subsequently serving as a schoolteacher in East Kingston and Merrimack. She first met her future husband, John Milton Hawks, in 1850. A native of New Hampshire, Hawks had earned his medical degree in 1847 and was operating an office and drug store in Manchester when they met. After an interesting courtship, the two married in 1854, and Esther soon began studying medicine with her husband and worked in his drugstore. However, she "was so determined," as historian Gerald Schwartz writes in his forward to her diaries, to become a doctor that she enrolled in the New England Female Medical College in Boston in 1855. She graduated two years later and returned to Manchester, trying to establish her own practice and also working in the family drugstore.

The relationship between Esther and John was an interesting one to say the least. The couple wholeheartedly embraced the abolitionist movement and were ardent supporters. John was into many social causes, including the suffrage movement, but was also later involved in land speculation and early settlements in the state of Florida. While he loved his wife, there is no doubt he was jealous of her pursuits, he later writing: "I wished Ette had never seen a medical book, or heard a lecture. It is not a business man-like worker a husband needs. It is a loving woman." Esther no doubt loved her husband, but she was also fiercely independent-minded. In 1861, she travelled to Washington, D.C., hoping to join the army in some medical capacity. However, no female doctors were being hired, and the head of the Army Nurse program, Dorothea Dix, rejected her for the program, she being too young and too attractive (according to the standards Dix had set) to be accepted. After her husband was accepted as a regimental surgeon in the Union Army, heading south to the Sea Islands of South Carolina, Esther stayed home to run the couple's drugstore and operate her own growing practice, as well as running a booming elixir business.

Anxious to help in any way she could, Esther Hill Hawks was accepted by the National Freedmen's Relief Association as a teacher and was sent south in October 1862. Here she rejoined her husband, working as a teacher and *de facto* army nurse. Later, she was employed as an assistant surgeon, and later still, for several weeks, was in charge of a hospital for black soldiers. Among those she treated were members of the famed Fifty-Fourth Massachusetts Regiment, a unit composed of African American soldiers that took heavy casualties in July 1863 after the assault on Fort Wagner on Morris Island. Of their care, she would write: "I endeavored with my whole heart, to make this dreary hospital life, as home—like as possible—and I was richly rewarded by their grateful thanks." Later, in 1864, the Hawks went with their regiment to Florida, treating the wounded after the Battle of Olustee. Her entire wartime career was devoted to not just caring medically for wounded black soldiers, but also for teaching both freed blacks and those that were serving in the Union Army.

At war's end, the Hawks made their way from South Carolina to Volusia County, Florida, followed by many of those whom Esther had treated in South Carolina. Here, on land provided by the government located near the Halifax River, they established the new settlement of Port Orange. Esther Hill Hawks, by 1866, had established the first racially integrated school in the state in the area later known as Freemanville. However, white families in the area were unhappy about her efforts, some withdrawing their children from school. The end of racial integration here came in 1869, when the school built by Esther was burned to the ground. Discouraged, Esther Hill Hawks moved back north, settling in Lynn, Massachusetts and building a thriving medical practice. Her husband, ever the wanderer, remained in Florida, but he would spend summers with Esther in Lynn, while she made the trip down to Florida in the winter months.

Though Esther did not live in the state, New Hampshire did not forget her, the New Hampshire Association of Military Surgeons making her an honorary member in 1899. After her death in 1906, one friend would later recall that "she never became a mere physician to the body; she has been quite active in the treatment of the soul and the development of character." Truer words were never spoken.

Esther Hill Hawkes, 1906,
Pine Grove Cemetery,
Manchester.

8

WOMEN OF TRAGEDY

Not every life story ends happily, and evidence of that fact, at least for some New Hampshire women, is readily evident in our local cemeteries. Beyond those deaths due to disease, illness, accident, and childbirth, most untimely manners of death go unrecorded—though they may exist, I have never seen a gravestone or monument specifying death by suicide or spousal abuse. But murder? Well, that is another case altogether and thus, with the penchant those in the Victorian Era had for the dramatic when it came to death, it is not surprising that some examples abound. Sadly, it is often the case, as will be seen below, that we know less about the victims than the perpetrators of these horrific deeds. It was true in the nineteenth century and remains largely true today. Of course, there are countless others whose lives are touched by tragedy, even if they themselves are not tragic figures. The ones included here are amazing stories with historical twists.

SALLY COCHRAN (1805-1833), OLD NORTH PEMBROKE CEMETERY, NORTH PEMBROKE

Can being kind and forgiving get you killed? Perhaps this was the case with young Sally Cochran. Of her life, we know very little. She was the youngest of four children of Moses and Jenny Cochran, and was named after their third child, who died in infancy in 1804. Born in Derry, she came with her family to Pembroke in 1819, and in November 1828, she married Chauncey Cochran, a local farmer.

The couple had two children, Sarah (born 1829) and a son, G. Newton (born 1830), as well as Chauncey's mother living with them. In 1830, there was another addition to the household, fifteen-year-old Abraham Prescott, who, as would be found out later, was a troubled boy. He worked as a hired hand and was said to be treated like a family member. There is no record that Prescott was any trouble at all, until January 1833, when he attacked Sally and Chauncey with an axe while they were sleeping. He subsequently claimed to have been sleepwalking when he attacked his hosts. Luckily, Sally and Chauncey survived the attack, no charges being filed because Sally placed no blame on Prescott, believing he did not mean to do what he had done. It was a kind decision by a kind woman, but one with fatal consequences.

Six months later, on June 23, a Sunday morning, Sally brought Abraham to a relative's field to pick strawberries while her husband stayed home. Shortly thereafter, Chauncey heard noises coming from the barn, and discovered Abraham Prescott inside alone and crying, with Sally nowhere in sight. Cochran got Abraham to tell him some of the story and had him take him to the field, where he found Sally, bloody and battered and still alive, but not for long. She had been beaten in the head with a wooden stake by Abraham Prescott while gathering strawberries and probably did not know what hit her.

Following her death, Prescott was taken into custody and charged with her murder. Two accounts emerged as to what had happened. The first was that Prescott was mentally deficient and had no memory of the attack. His defense lawyers claimed that his sleepwalking, which had been a problem since he was a child, was indicative of his condition, and that he had been treated before for mental problems. On the other hand, under questioning from the jail-keeper, Prescott admitted that he had made an "improper advance" against Sally and was, of course, rebuffed by her in an angry manner and would tell her husband what had happened. Believing he would go to jail for the incident, he killed Sally in order to cover up his actions. Later on, Prescott recanted this confession, saying he had made it up. The jury heard both sides, and convicted Prescott for murder.

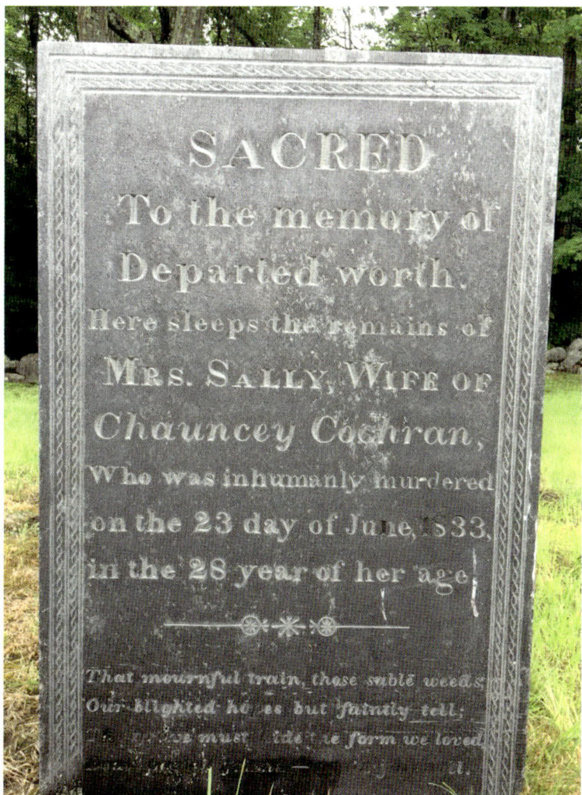

Sally Cochran, 1833, Old North Pembroke Cemetery, Pembroke.

When it was discovered that the jurors in the case had improperly discussed the case, resulting in a mistrial, Prescott was brought to trial again in 1835, two years after Sally was laid to rest. He was again found guilty and sentenced to hang. Though there were calls to commute Prescott's sentence, eventually, in January 1836, he was put to death. To this day, the murder case remains a landmark one when it comes to the legal justice system and the mentally handicapped and how practices have evolved. More immediately, the Prescott case was also a factor that led to the establishment of New Hampshire's first state mental hospital and its mental health system.

One gets the sense, perhaps, that Sally Cochran would have been sympathetic to Prescott and approved of a commutation of his sentence, but for her husband, this was certainly not the case. The gravestone he had erected for Sally makes clear, and understandably so, his views on his wife's demise. Afterwards, perhaps due to the great publicity surrounding the case, Chauncey Cochran moved his family to Corinth, Maine, to start a new life. He gave up farming to be a shopkeeper, married again, and fathered seven children.

SEVILLA JONES (1836–1854), NEW BOSTON CEMETERY, NEW BOSTON

If ever there was a case where the killer got more sympathetic attention and press than the victim, the murder of seventeen-year-old Sevilla Jones in New Boston is one of the most egregious examples. Sevilla's mother, Sarah Battles Jones, however, would have none of that. Sevilla Jones was born in New Boston, the daughter of Sarah and George Jones. The family was well off, George having a good farm, which his sons helped to work.

Of Sevilla's life, we know little; her father died just months before she did in 1853, and she was a student at the time of her murder. She was walking her younger brother to school on the morning of January 13, 1854 (yes, that was a Friday), and when in the area of Joe English Hill, twenty-three-year-old Henry Sargent came up to her with gun hidden in hand. Sevilla offered a pleasant greeting, he responded by shooting her four times in the head, then turning the gun on himself. She died instantly, while he lingered for several hours.

The town doctor was said to be so distraught over the death of Sevilla that he refused to treat Sargent. So, it was a murder-suicide event, but why? Sargent, whose family were neighbors to the Joneses, had worked as a woodsman and actually left behind a suicide note/will, subsequently published in full. It detailed his affection for Sevilla, which she at first returned, but later on spurned, despite his heavy advances. Sargent blamed her mother and others in town for Sevilla turning away from him. There are also intimations about money, that Henry may not have been considered good enough for her by Sevilla's mother, and a rival suitor, probably Ebenezer Bartlett. He also asks that some of the things he gave to Sevilla, including a Bible and miniature portraits, be returned to his parents.

Sargent had apparently plotted the murder-suicide for weeks, and even had the gall to ask Sevilla's mother that they be buried side by side, "and put on our gravestones what we died for." This line Sarah Battles Jones would take to heart, making her daughter's gravesite to this day a well-known local attraction. Understand: this story was a big one, it having all the classic elements, a distraught lover, a young beauty, and a dramatic death scene. The story made the papers even in New York and, sadly, most of it focused on Sargent and his motivations, and almost nothing was written of Sevilla Jones.

When it came time to create a gravestone for Sevilla, stonecutter Moses Davis of Nashua was chosen for the job. Sarah made clear the inscription she wanted, "Murdered by Henry N. Sargent…. Thus fell this lovely blooming daughter. By the revengeful hand-a malicious Henry. When on her way to school he met her. And with a six self cocked pistol shot her." Davis asked if that was what she really wanted, and that she might regret it later on. As you can see, Sarah did not change her mind, and so the gravestone was put in place over her daughter's final resting place for all to see. Moreover, she also saw to it that Henry Sargent was not buried anywhere close to Sevilla, thus denying her murderer one of his stated wishes. Thus, this story is not just one about the tragic death or a young woman, but also about her protective and grieving mother.

Above left: Sevilla Jones, 1854, New Boston Cemetery, New Boston.

Above right: Sarah (Jones) Battles, 1894, the mother of Sevilla Jones, New Boston Cemetery, New Boston.

KATHERINE SCOTT CUMMINGS (1842–1862) AND MARY SOPHIA FULLER SCOTT (1830–1862), VILLAGE CEMETERY, PETERBOROUGH, AND JULIA WAKEFIELD DORT (1832–1862), WOODLAND CEMETERY, KEENE

On the bottom of the bronze tablet on the Soldiers Monument in Peterborough, there can be found the names of two women, a rare addition on such monuments in New Hampshire when it was created in June 1870. At the monument's dedication, it was said of these women "recognize these as the former friends of soldiers, and also that they lost their lives within the army lines … do not forget them, but hold them in tender remembrance … decorate their graves. So also, in yonder bronze we have cut their names, as fit companion names to go down in posterity with the names of our town's brave and fallen heroes." This is a story of random and capricious death amidst a great national tragedy, the Civil War, that was then playing out. And it involved three women actually, not just the two listed, as well as one child.

The youngest of the women in this story was Catherine "Katie" Scott Cummings, the daughter of prominent Peterborough townsfolk Sarah Wilson Scott and James Scott. Little is known of her early life, but in December 1861, at the beginning of the Civil War, she married John Cummings. The other woman noted on the Peterborough Soldiers Monument is Mary Sophia Fuller Scott, the daughter of Mary Scott Fuller and Charles Fuller. In July 1848, she married Charles Scott and they would have two children, Charles and Ella, who died in infancy. The third woman in our story who would share the same fate is Julia Nancy Wakefield Dort of Keene. The daughter of Nancy and James Wakefield, she married town druggist Obed Dort in October 1851. The couple would have three children, including Arthur and Mary, who died in infancy in 1861.

All of these women were brought together by the Civil War and the formation of the Sixth New Hampshire Regiment of Volunteers in 1861. All of their husbands were leaders in the regiment at its formation, Charles Scott serving as major, Obed Dort as a company captain, and John Cummings as a first lieutenant under Dort. The regiment departed Keene for Washington, D.C., on Christmas Day 1861, twenty-four days after Katie and John Cummings were married. There would be no honeymoon. The regiment took part in operations in the Carolinas from January–July 1862 before moving to Newport News, Virginia, for a brief respite.

The first to arrive there was Mary Scott; her husband, Charles, was sick with malaria and she helped care for him. Katie Cummings, who badly missed her new husband, travelled south to Baltimore in the company of Julia Dort and her son, Arthur, who was six years old. Here they met Major Dort and went by ship to Newport News. Katie Cummings missed seeing her husband as part of the regiment was on the move again and he was among them. We can only imagine her great disappointment. Captain Dort, too, after arriving at Newport News, was sent off with his men, leaving his wife and son in company with the other women. All the women and the Dort boy remained in Newport News until the morning of August 13, 1862, when the sick and wounded of the regiment, including Major Scott, as well as those from other regiments, were put aboard the steamer *West Point*, destined for a hospital in Washington, D.C. Katie Cummings came along in hopes of finding her husband John, writing him a letter which stated, in part, "I cannot go home without making one more effort to see you." The steamer departed for Washington with some 279 people aboard, all of them ill soldiers except the three women and Captain Dort's son, headed up the Potomac River. They would never make their final destination.

At 9 p.m. that evening, the steamer collided with another transport vessel, the down-bound *George Peabody*, and at first it was not thought that the steamer was in peril. However, things quickly changed and the heavily laden *West Point* began to take on water. Some of the crew abandoned ship right away leaving the passengers to their fate. Through the efforts of nearby vessels, about 200 people were rescued, but seventy-nine were drowned when the ship sank, including all the women and Arthur Dort. Sergeant Parker of the Sixth New Hampshire helped Julia Dort and her boy in their cabin below and got them and the other two women to the upper deck of the ship with the help of Dr. James Newell, a New Hampshire native. The doctor told the women to stay by him and be calm and he would try to save them. He held Arthur Dort as the water rose but, sadly, with the great amount of people on the deck, it eventually collapsed, they and many others being thrown into the water. While Major Scott survived by holding onto a part of the sunken ship until daybreak, the women were thrown into the water and drifted away.

Two days later, the body of Dr. Newell and that of one of the women, possibly Mary Scott, were found clinging together. The body of Mary Sophia Scott and the other women washed ashore in Confederate territory and were given a decent burial by them. Her husband tried to get permission to recover the women's bodies, but was denied such. However, the father of Katie Scott Cummings came to Washington to get permission to bring the bodies back home, and after several meetings, including an impromptu one with President Lincoln, finally received permission and accomplished his solemn mission. Thus, it was that the burial sites of his beloved daughter "Katie" and Mary Scott can be visited today in Peterborough, as well as that for Julia Dort and her son in Keene, accidental casualties of the Civil War.

JOSIE A. LANGMAID (1857–1875), BUCK STREET CEMETERY, PEMBROKE

This young woman is perhaps one of the most famous murder victims in all of New Hampshire history. Part of this is due to the heinous nature of the crime and the subsequent discovery that its perpetrator was, in fact, a serial killer. Josie Langmaid was the daughter of Mary Ann Marden Langmaid and James F. Langmaid, the oldest of their four children. She was seventeen years old and a student at Pembroke Academy on the fall day it was discovered that she was missing, October 4, 1875.

Normally, Josie walked to school from her home and through the woods with her friend, Lilla Fowler, or might accompany her brother, Waldo, but on this day, she was running late, and so made the walk alone. She greeted one townsman on the way, but was never seen again. When she failed to appear home that evening after having never arrived at school, the family and a large search party were gathered to look for her. Long after dark, in a wooded swamp, her lifeless body was found. Her clothes were tattered and bloody and, shockingly, her head was missing. It was discovered some distance away later the next morning, her face battered and beaten. Whoever it may have been that raped and killed the popular young woman, Josie had put up a fight.

The town and, indeed, all of New Hampshire and New England were shocked by the terrible crime, it being reported in newspapers far beyond. The search was on for the perpetrator, with one man jailed early on, but soon attention was focused on

Above left: Katie Cummings, 1862, Village Cemetery, Peterborough.

Above right: Portrait of Katie Cummings, *c.* 1861. (*Courtesy Monadnock Center for History and Culture*)

Above left: Mary Sophia Scott, 1862, Village Cemetery, Peterborough.

Above right: Portrait photo, Mary Sophia Scott. (*Courtesy of Monadnock Center for History and Culture*)

a drifter from Quebec, Canada, named Joseph LaPage, who had come to Pembroke from St. Albans, Vermont. It turns out that just the year before in July 1874, a young schoolteacher named Mariette Ball had been murdered there in a similarly brutal fashion, and though LaPage was a suspect, there was not enough evidence against him. Officials in St. Albans wrote to Pembroke authorities asking that they take a good hard look at him. As it turns out, there was more than enough evidence found linking LaPage to Josie Langmaid's murder. Subsequently dubbed the "French Monster," LaPage was convicted of her killing after two trials and was hanged at Concord on March 15, 1878. Before his death, he admitted to killing Langmaid, and afterwards it was discovered that he had killed two other women in Canada.

As for Josie Langmaid, she was laid to rest in the Buck Street Cemetery, soon to be followed by her brother, Waldo, who died just over two months later due to disease. Her sad demise might be largely forgotten today, except for the fact that the town, in true Victorian fashion, erected a large monument at the site where Langmaid's body was found, complete with details about where her head was discovered. This monument seems a bit strange, and it is even a bit unnerving visiting the site, but it has served the purpose of keeping the memory of the victim "alive," while her heavily publicized killer has faded into obscurity. Located across the street from Three Rivers School, the monument is known by every child in Pembroke who has gone to school here and Josie Langmaid's death is somewhat of a legend, though many who live in town have passed the monument site by without knowing its historical significance.

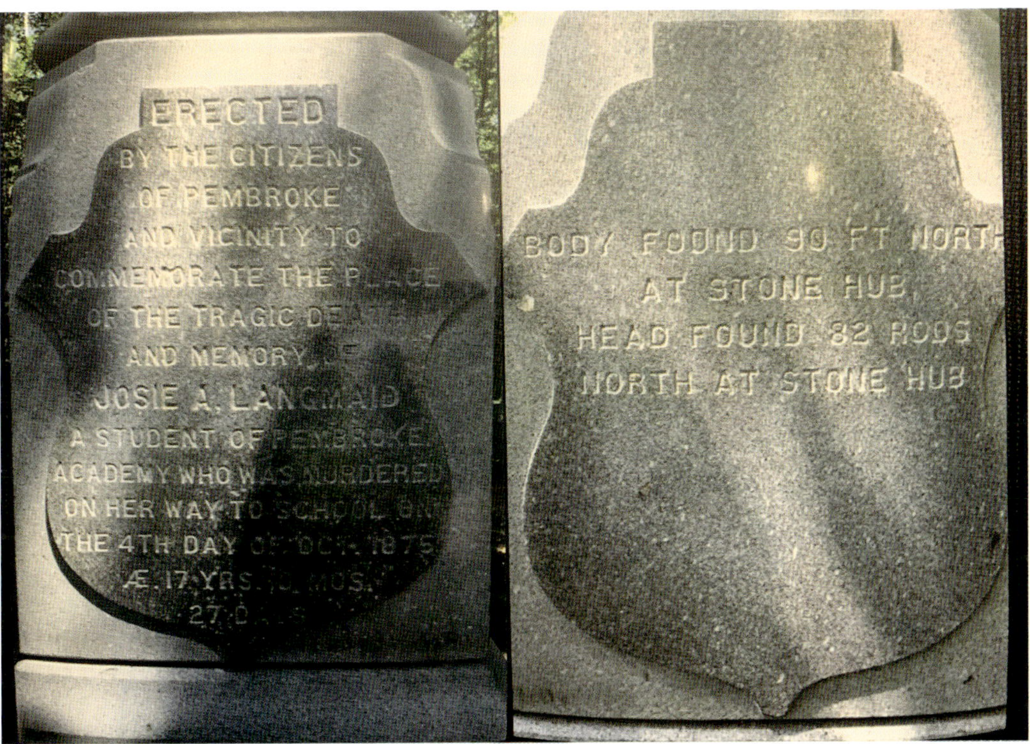

Inscriptions on the monument erected near the site where Josie Langmaid's body was discovered.

Langmaid Family monument, Josie Langmaid (1875), Buck Street Cemetery, Pembroke.

Lucy Lambert Hale Chandler (1841–1915), Pine Hill Cemetery, Dover

Imagine, if you will, the woman who has it all—looks, personality, intelligence, and social status. She could have married a New Hampshire boy, but instead has romances (or near-romances) with the son of a president, a future Supreme Court justice, a close advisor to a president, and even an actor. Later, though, as her life changes, she returns to marry her local suitor of years gone by. That, in a nutshell, is the life of Lucy Hale. However, the devil is in the details, as the saying goes, and those details make for a historically fascinating life that was intertwined with one of our country's greatest tragedies.

Lucy Lambert Hale was born in Dover, the daughter of Lucy Lambert Hale. Her father, John Parker Hale, was a prominent New Hampshire political figure who served as a U.S. senator from 1847–1853 and 1855–1865, and even ran for president in 1852. Most notably, Hale was a staunch abolitionist and was a prominent and persistent critic of the Lincoln administration, especially the Department of the Navy. As unpopular as John Hale was in many circles in Washington, such was not the case with his young daughter. Indeed, from an early age, the boys were drawn to her: at the age of twelve, a young man from Concord, William Chandler, a law student at Harvard, was writing her love poems. At the age of seventeen, she met future Supreme Court Justice Oliver Wendel Holmes, Jr., while vacationing with her family in Maine, he writing her several "expressive" letters expressing his romantic desires.

Lucy was then attending a boarding school in Hanover, New Hampshire, but soon transferred to a boarding school in Cambridge, Massachusetts, not far from the campus of Harvard University, where Holmes was a student. While she moved on from Holmes (though they remained life-long friends), here she met Robert Todd Lincoln, the son of the soon-to-be-president. While the two never dated, they did socialize and become life-long friends, though her father held out hopes that the two would marry. During the Civil War, Lucy lived with her family in the National Hotel in Washington, D.C. By day she did great work for the U.S. Sanitary Commission, whose female workers helped raise money for soldier relief efforts, as well as serving as nurses in federally run hospitals, and many other duties.

Early in the war, she even visited the front lines with her mother, riding in the back of an ambulance. In her off-hours, however, Lucy, described by historian Richmond Morcom as having "clear skin, large blue eyes, dark hair, and a stunning figure," was one of the belles of Washington society and had many suitors. She had a personality that was both alluring and enigmatic to men, it being "a subtle brew of flattery, teasing, and cajoling; of rapt attention disturbingly laced with hints of indifference, and even, now and then, a touch of cruelty." Among her suitors was President Lincoln's personal secretary, John Hay. He would later write to her, in 1869, that "You know how I love and admire you. I do not understand you, nor hope to, nor even wish to. You would lose to me something of your indefinable fascination if I knew exactly what you meant."

Lucy's flirt with tragedy began on Valentine's Day in 1862, when she received a romantic letter from one of the most famed actors of the day, John Wilkes Booth. What followed was a courtship that started slowly at first, but by March 1865, the two, who were widely seen together about town, were full on in love and were, in fact, "secretly" engaged, though rumors about the betrothal were widespread. However,

Booth had other matters at hand and was by this time actively involved in the plot to kidnap Lincoln, which soon morphed into a more deadly plan. Indeed, it was through a ticket he received from Lucy that he attended Lincoln's second inauguration, though most historians believe that Lucy was blissfully unaware of any of Booth's devious dealings, or even his political sympathies. By April, however, matters between Booth and Lucy were strained, perhaps because Booth saw her dancing one night with Robert Todd Lincoln. It has also been speculated that perhaps his attention towards Lucy was distracted by his involvement in the plot against Lincoln. However, there may have been one other factor that drove Booth away from Lucy and even more headlong into what would turn out to be an assassination plot.

When her father lost his senate seat in the election of 1864, Hale was subsequently appointed to be the U.S. Minister to Spain by Lincoln in 1865 and would soon be moving there, taking Lucy with him and leaving Booth behind. On the day that President Lincoln was assassinated by Booth, Lucy is even thought to have been studying Spanish with Robert Todd Lincoln and John Hay. After the assassination, with Washington in an uproar, Lucy could hardly believe that it had been her fiancé who was responsible. When John Wilkes Booth was subsequently hunted down and killed by Union soldiers in Virginia on April 26, 1865, among the items found in his coat-pocket were the photos of five women, one of whom was Lucy Hale. This evidence, combined with the fact that Lucy's relationship with Booth was widely known, put Senator Hale in a difficult situation, he even taking out public advertisements denying their relationship.

Whether Lucy Hale may have had any insights into Booth's actions or how the plot against Lincoln evolved will never be known as Secretary of War Edwin Stanton made sure that she would never take part as a witness in the trial of Booth's fellow conspirators. Instead, Lucy Hale went off to Spain with her father, leaving Washington behind. Here she remained from 1865–70, and while she still attracted attention from suitors, attended balls, travelled throughout Europe, and even visited sites in Paris with her old friends John Hay and Oliver Wendell Holmes, she never married. She lived in Dover upon her return to the United States, caring for her sick father.

After John Hale's death in 1873, Lucy received attention once again from an old suitor, William Chandler, who had once been married but was now a widower. The two married in 1874, with Chandler serving in Washington as secretary of the Navy and U.S. senator, and Lucy his faithful and supportive wife. The couple would have one child, John Parker Chandler, born in 1875. When Lucy died in 1915, she was buried beside her father in the Hale family plot, while her husband, who died two years later, was buried in his hometown of Concord.

Right: Lucy Hale Chandler, 1915, Pine Hill Cemetery, Dover. The monument for her father is in the background.

Below: Items found on the body of John Wilkes Booth after his death. Lucy Hale's photograph is second from the left. (*Photo by Carol M. Highsmith, courtesy of the Library of Congress*)

9

WOMEN IN BUSINESS

New Hampshire women have long been involved in financial pursuits since the earliest days when the colony was established in the 1600s. At first, opportunities were severely limited both by societal tradition and established law, but nonetheless, women persevered and showed their entrepreneurial spirit in many different ways. Some, as we have seen previously, sold hand-sewn goods, took in laundry, or operated as tavern-keepers, but others found additional ways to monetize their skills. The women listed below are a small but fascinating sampling of some of the other economic pursuits that women engaged in as opportunities slowly increased throughout the nineteenth century.

RACHEL SOUTHARD (1748-1823), HORSE MEADOW CEMETERY, NORTH HAVERHILL

While combing through dozens of New Hampshire town and county histories written in the nineteenth century, I found mention of a lot of "founding fathers," with few women mentioned. However, every so often, a woman gets mentioned, one of them being Rachel Cummings Southard.

Rachel was likely born in Windham County, Connecticut, probably in the town of Ashford. It was here, during the American Revolution, that she married Thomas Southard on March 23, 1778 at the Congregational Church. Soon thereafter, in 1780, the first of the couple's five children, was born. The young couple would subsequently move to New Hampshire, settling in Acworth by 1785, and later on in Hanover, where Thomas Southard bought a farm. Unfortunately, the title for this land was flawed and the family lost everything and moved to Charlestown, where Thomas died in 1790. This left Rachel Southward with five young children and a family to support all on her own. While many women in her situation would marry again, not Rachel Southard—as the *Gazetteer of Grafton County, New Hampshire* tells us: "Mrs. Southard was a woman of great energy and industry, endowed with a brain fertile in resources, and, by her artistic and skillful work in weaving linen of various designs, was enabled to support her fatherless children."

Virtually nothing else is known about this "worthy" woman, but that single sentence, really, paints a picture of her life. She did it all, raising three sons, James (the oldest), and twins, Moses and Aaron, and daughters, Eliza and Lucinda. Moses and Aaron moved to Haverhill in 1822, purchasing 500 acres of land, "one of the finest farms on the Connecticut River." It was here that Rachel Southard lived the final days of her life.

SUSANNA MASON SMITH (1763-1845), DARTMOUTH COLLEGE CEMETERY, HANOVER

Born in Boston, Susanna Mason Smith was the daughter of Hannah Symmes Mason and Captain David Mason. Her father was one who had "a nice perception of aesthetic beauty" and even studied portrait painting in his youth, but is best known as a prominent artillery officer during the American Revolution.

Susanna was the couple's youngest child and well-remembered in her old age the Revolutionary War period in Boston, where she and her older sister, Hannah, helped melt "domestic utensils" and pewter plates and turn them into musket balls, as well as making powder cartridges. Susanna married Rev. John Smith in 1785 and was his second wife. The couple would have two sons. Rev. Smith gained his degree from Dartmouth College in 1778 and was subsequently a professor of languages there until his death. Smith was very close to Dartmouth founder Eleazar Wheeler and also served as college librarian. Smith brought Susanna "to Hanover as a bride on horseback," it being said "that in the course of her early married life [she] made the same journey five times," travelling back and forth from Boston.

Rev. Smith also operated the Dartmouth College bookstore in a room in the couple's house with Susanna's help. It is quite likely that Susanna was the major operator of the bookstore due to her husband's extensive college duties, so it is not surprising that, after his death in 1809, she continued to operate the bookstore for another three or four years on her own. This makes her one of the first, if not the first, female bookstore owners in the state. As the historians of Dartmouth College and Hanover would later note, Susanna Mason Smith "was a most estimable woman, and highly esteemed at Hanover." After her husband's death, she would write a memoir of her husband's life, which she completed in 1843, though the manuscript was never published. While her husband was never a popular preacher or teacher among the student body at Dartmouth, Susanna may have more than made up for his deficiencies, her gravestone noting that she had "a long life practicing all the virtues, and endearing herself to very many by her kind and gentle offices."

HANNAH DAVIS (1784-1863), OLD BURYING GROUND, JAFFREY CENTER

It is an old proverb that "Necessity is the mother of invention," and in the case of Hannah Davis, truer words were never spoken. She was the daughter of Hannah Eaton Davis and Peter Davis, born five years or so before the couple married in January 1789. Her father was a wooden clock-maker—it is not known when Peter Davis died, but it was probably before 1800, as the census for that year shows Hannah Eaton Davis as the head of a household that included a young boy and a young girl, her daughter, Hannah, as well

Above left: Rachel Southard, 1823, Horse Meadow Cemetery, North Haverhill.

Above right: Susannah Smith, 1845, Dartmouth College Cemetery, Hanover.

as an older male (possibly her grandfather). Life was no doubt difficult and we know not how Hannah and her mother supported themselves, but it may be that Hannah had learned a little bit about wood-working from her father (or perhaps she learned it all on her own) and may have begun making band boxes to support the household.

However, it was after the death of her mother in May 1818 that Hannah Davis, now a spinster at the age of thirty-six, was really on her own. And that is when her band box business would really take off. Now, you might ask, "What is a band box?" Well, these were circular or oval boxes, usually made of cheap pasteboard, with a removeable top and originally, in earlier times, used to store men's collar bands. However, in 1800s New England, they were a women's fashion accessory, used to store or transport hair ribbons, beads, gloves, or any type of personal articles. Most were covered with period wallpaper for a decorative effect and though relatively few of the countless numbers that were made have survived to this day, they were always considered a cherished part of a women's belongings.

Hannah Davis, however, was an innovator; having come up with the idea of selling this popular item, she resolved to make hers out of the best material possible—wood. To that end, she invented a wood-cutting machine, operated by a foot pedal, which cut thins strips of wood off a log, about one-eighth of an inch thick, which could be bended to form the sides of an oval band box. The bottom and lids of her boxes were made of thin slices of pine wood, components fastened together using small nails. Hannah gained her materials by scoping out suitable trees in and around Jaffrey, and then arranged to purchase them from the landowners, subsequently paying someone to cut it down and transport it to her yard, where it was then cut into sections.

Not only was Davis smart, but she was tough, for the work of converting logs to band box materials was not easy. At first, her boxes were small, but as time went on, they grew in size. Hannah was a true entrepreneur who did it all by herself. Not only did she cover her boxes with wallpaper scraps, which she either purchased or bartered for, she also lined the interior with newsprint from newspapers, many religious in nature, she obtained locally, also by barter. Realizing there were bigger markets for her wares beyond Jaffrey (where there were only so many women), she bought a prairie-schooner type wagon and would load it with her boxes, travelling throughout the area, including the mill towns of Manchester and Lowell, Massachusetts, where there were hundreds of young women working with wages to spend.

Davis, who was known as Aunt Hannah to all who knew her, was also fair in her pricing, local historians stating that her largest boxes fetched 50 cents, while her smallest but 12 cents, a price range of $3.50 to about $15 in 2021 dollars. Most importantly, Hannah Davis knew the power of branding and marketing—every one of her boxes carried a paper label affixed to the inside lid, which stated "Warranted Nailed Band Boxes, manufactured by Hannah Davis, East Jaffrey, N.H." It is quite likely that Davis stored up her raw materials and worked on creating many of her boxes during the winter months by the fireside when the weather was bad. However, hers was an all-year

Above left: Hannah Davis, 1863, Old Burying Ground, Jaffrey Center.

Above right: Portrait of Hannah Davis, 1855. (*Courtesy Cheshire County Historical Society*)

business, with Davis out selling her wares in the winter months using a horse-drawn sleigh. No matter how she did it, Hannah Davis did it well, and her boxes were a popular commodity throughout the region for years, known for their fine construction. To this day, surviving examples of her boxes sell for thousands of dollars to collectors.

Later in life, she broke her hip and was unable to support herself financially. Because she was a beloved character in town, known for her story-telling and the funny songs she sang, the townsfolk of East Jaffrey were always there to help. The Baptist Church where she was a devout member built her a house on Main Street, while farmers would donate wood for heating, and school-boys were sent to chop it into firewood, afterwards invited in for dinner and a round of entertainment. Hannah Davis was truly a one of a kind business-woman in her day.

PERSIS FOSTER EAMES ALBEE (1836-1914), EVERGREEN CEMETERY, WINCHESTER

In today's retail world, where personal care products and cosmetics can be found at any big box retailer, it is all about convenience and customer service. Way back in the 1880s, nobody understood this more than Persis Albee. And because of her skill set, business acumen, and her uncanny ability to build a sales force, she helped take a small direct to consumer company, and set it on the way to what it has become today, a company with over $5 billion in sales annually.

Persis Foster Eames was born in Newry, Maine, the daughter of Miranda Howe Eames and Alexander Eames and the second youngest of their five daughters. Little is known of her early life, but by 1860, she was working as a teacher, and by 1866, she was living in Williamsburg, New York, and married to Ellery Albee, a lawyer from Winchester, New Hampshire. The couple would move to Winchester, New Hampshire, within several years, building their family. Persis Albee's husband, a lawyer, was a native and was involved in state politics for a few years before the couple opened a general store in their home. Because they lived near the railroad depot, and the only public telephone was in their store, they did a good business, though times were sometimes hard and they could not even pay their town taxes.

Persis ran the family store well, being "courteous, personable, and willing to meet the demands of her customers," and had staff that was excellently trained. No doubt to help boost her family's income, Persis worked as book peddler for the Union Publishing House beginning about 1879, making a commission on what she sold locally. She was a natural at selling, but when her boss David McConnell hit on the idea of handing out small vials of perfume to encourage women to buy the books, it soon became clear that women really were more interested in the perfumes. To that end, in 1886, McConnell started the California Perfume Company in New York, with Persis Albee, a widow by 1885, as his sole agent. Not only did Albee push sales for the new perfume company by building a display in the family store, but she also took to the road as a travelling sales person.

While McConnell may have come up with the idea of marketing direct to women, it was Persis Albee who made it happen—not only did she grow the business through her personal sales efforts, but she was so good at it that she was soon promoted to manager, put in charge of hiring and training other women. It was because of Albee's hard work and the business model that she put into place that the California Perfume Company expanded at a rapid rate and soon included in its offerings new perfumes and other personal care articles. Albee was so important to their success that she was called the "Mother of the California Perfume Company," and was known for her "unfailing integrity." She not only trained over 5,000 sales associates from 1886–1898, but she also helped develop the company's product offerings.

Many years later, after Albee's death, the name of the company was changed to Avon, which today remains an iconic cosmetics brand and relies on the same woman-to-woman sales model that Persis Albee developed all those years ago. It is for that reason that Persis is often referred to as the first "Avon lady" in history. However, Albee is not just important for developing what would become a global company; she also developed a path by which women could become financially independent, a vital aspect of the woman's suffrage movement.

Of course, Albee was also active in Winchester and was a true community leader, teaching Sunday school and being president of the Winchester Literary Guild. Indeed, it was because of her community presence that Albee was a sales success, being "dressed in her elegant clothing and with her friendly manner, Persis was a welcome sight. She was not considered a nuisance, but as a "friendly neighbor come to call." In her later years, with her health on the decline, Persis Albee moved in with her daughter, Ellen Albee Day, in Baldwinville, Massachusetts, here dying from a chronic heart condition in 1914. Though long gone, Persis Foster Eames Albee's pioneering efforts live on in the countless different forms in which woman's businesses thrive today.

Albee Family monument, Persis Albee (1914), Evergreen Cemetery, Winchester.

10

TWENTIETH-CENTURY PIONEERS

In our final chapter, the women discussed below are significant for doing things that no woman, either in New Hampshire or beyond, had ever done before. All were women that broke barriers, some doing so in quiet fashion, others doing so in a very public spotlight. The effects the accomplishments had on their own lives varied; for several, their achievements came at the ultimate cost, while for others the significance of their achievements has, unfairly, faded with time. All of them are worthy of remembrance not only for what they have done, but also for the effects they have had on future generations of women.

FRANCES GLESSNER LEE (1878–1962), MAPLE STREET CEMETERY, BETHLEHEM

The story of how the daughter of a wealthy Midwest industrialist came to be named an honorary New Hampshire State Police captain, the first woman in the country ever to achieve such a position, is a fascinating one.

Frances "Fanny" Glessner was born in Chicago, the daughter of Sarah Frances Macbeth Glessner and her husband, John Glessner. He was a farm implement manufacturer and was a key player in the merger of his company with another to create the farm machinery giant International Harvester, serving as the newly formed company's vice-president. The couple would have three children, one who died infancy, and Fanny was the youngest and only daughter. Her mother was a fascinating and very creative woman and was known for her piano playing, knitting and seamstress skills, her interest in bee-keeping, but was also a silversmith. Her silverware hallmark included the letter "G" surrounding a honey bee, a symbol that was also used on the family's grave markers in Bethlehem.

Fanny early on came to know New Hampshire when, in 1884, her father had built the family's summer estate, known as "The Rocks," in Bethlehem, to provide relief for her older brother George's hay fever condition. The family would often spend five months or more a year here in her early years, with George and his wife moving here full-time in 1916. Fanny, after her schooling was over, toured Europe for over a year with her aunt before returning to high society in Chicago. She married lawyer Blewett Lee in 1898 and with him had three children, John (born 1898), Frances (born 1903), and Martha (born 1906). However, the couple divorced in 1914, probably in part because of Frances' creative pursuits, in which her husband had no interest. She would subsequently manage a sailor's and soldier's home in Boston during World War I, and later became an antiques dealer in New Hampshire, moving to Bethlehem permanently in 1938.

During her time in Boston, she became interested in the science of "legal medicine," today known as "forensics," through her friendship with Dr. George Magrath, the Suffolk County Medical Examiner and an old friend of her brother. In 1931, she helped create a chair in legal medicine, and in 1936 provided the department with a sizeable endowment of $250,000. Further, in 1934, she donated over 1,000 books to found the Magrath Library of Legal Medicine. However, Frances was not just a supporter of the new science of forensics and crime scene examination, she also played an active part through the creation of her "Nutshell Studies of Unexplained Death" models. Using the artistic skills she had learned from her mother, Frances recreated the details of twenty actual challenging crime scenes in miniature in painstaking fashion, thereby giving investigators a new tool in the field of criminology. Her goal was to "convict the guilty, clear the innocent, and find the truth in a nutshell." These nutshell models, developed by Lee after investigating the actual crime scenes and pouring over autopsies and other investigative records, were first used to train detectives and other police investigators during week-long seminars that she conducted twice a year, and were later used by students at Harvard until the department was closed in 1966. The models, of which eighteen still survive, were subsequently acquired by the Maryland Medical Examiner's Office and are still used to this day as a teaching tool at annual seminars, the solution to each nutshell remaining a secret.

Above left: Frances Glessner Lee, 1962, Maple Street Cemetery, Bethlehem.

Above right: Nutshell Study of Unexplained Death; The Red Bedroom Murder, detail, 1944, by Frances Glessner Lee. (*Photo courtesy of Lorie Shaull*)

Frances Lee's works are so important—not to mention fascinating—that they were even displayed at the Smithsonian Museum in 2017–18. It was in 1943, as Lee's work was growing in prominence, that she was made an honorary New Hampshire State Police captain, quite the honor for a Chicago-born socialite. Her status combined with her forensics knowledge also made her a name in the literary field, she becoming the friend of crime novelist Earle Stanley Gardiner. He was one of the attendees of her seminars and was the creator of character Perry Mason, later turned into a popular televisions series. Gardner even dedicated one of his novels, *The Case of the Dubious Bride Groom*, to Lee. It is important to remember that she was not just a pioneer in a new field of criminal investigation, but was also a woman working in what had previously been a man's world. So, the next time you are watching your favorite crime drama, give a thought to Frances Glessner Lee, for she is the one who started it all.

GRACE METALIOUS (1924-1964), SMITH MEETING HOUSE CEMETERY, GILMANTON

When we talk about those pioneering New Hampshire women who have broken barriers, there is no one that did it in such a bold and shocking manner as Grace Metalious. She did not just break barriers, and defy social norms to the shock (and delight) of many, she bulldozed them down. However, while she quickly gained international fame and notoriety beyond her wildest dreams, she just as quickly, like a passing comet, flamed out and was gone in a flash. Such was the tragic arc of her life.

She was born Marie Grace DeRepentigny in Manchester, the daughter of Laurette and Alfred DeRepentigny, of French-Canadian stock, her mother a dental assistant, her father a printer. Grace started writing as a young child, her favorite place being her aunt's bathtub, to escape the realities of her broken home. She continued to write even as a young woman, marrying her high-school boyfriend, George Metalious, the son of Greek immigrants, in 1942. Their subsequent life together was far from ideal—they were separated early on when George enlisted to fight in World War II, and after he came home, despite three children, both had affairs. For Grace Metalious, according to writer Michael Callahan, "Writing was neither hobby nor diversion, but lifeline."

By the early 1950s, the couple was living in poverty in Gilmanton, with George going to school on the G.I. Bill, while Grace stayed home and, leaving her children to fend for themselves, feverishly wrote a novel, which she titled *The Tree and the Blossom*, a scandalous story about a small New Hampshire town. For her novel, Grace based her characters, in part, on the people of Gilmanton, including Barbara Roberts, a young woman who killed her father after suffering years of sexual abuse, a shocking case that rocked the town in 1946–7. While Metalious had submitted a prior manuscript for publication through her agent, it was ignored. However, her newest work, after passing through several hands, was eagerly accepted by publisher Kitty Messner, the name changed to *Peyton Place*, the fictional New Hampshire town that was the setting of the novel. With its publication in 1956, Grace Metalious rocked the literary scene in America, selling 60,000 copies within ten days and remaining on *The New York Times* Bestseller List for a whopping fifty-nine weeks. While the literary critics panned the novel for its language and overt sexual scenes, for Americans it was a guilty pleasure,

Grace Metalious, 1964, Smith
Meeting House Cemetery, Gilmanton.

even in Gilmanton, whose residents were outraged at the thinly-veiled references to the town. Indeed, the term "Peyton Place" to this day has become a synonym for small-town scandal and drama.

However racy Grace Metalious' book may have been, it has also been recognized by later generations of literary critics and historians as a groundbreaking work of feminism, a book which explores female sexuality, as well as the changing times of 1950s America. So popular was Metalious' work that it was later turned in a movie, a prime-time television show, and, later, a day-time soap opera. However, while Metalious would release a follow-up book, *Return to Peyton Place* (1959), her life would never be the same and she never achieved the happiness she had sought since childhood. Not only did her agent take advantage of Metalious, but she also spent her hard-earned royalties lavishly and her personal life was ruined. Already a drinker before gaining fame, Metalious drank even more, and it would cost her dearly. Just eight years after the release of *Peyton Place*, Grace Metalious died in a Boston hospital due to cirrhosis of the liver at the age of forty.

The Metalious legacy in New Hampshire is a complicated one; residents in the town of Gilmanton despised *Peyton Place* for years and its author's name was never brought up in polite conversation. Perhaps things have changed in the ensuing five decades, but it is telling that to this day there is no historical marker of any kind in the town to note this pioneer-author.

RUTH FERRIS COREY (1894–1972), PINE GROVE CEMETERY, MANCHESTER

New Hampshire women have had a long history of serving as nurses during our nation's war, starting way back in the Revolutionary War with Molly Stark, but those women who served during World War I are perhaps the most forgotten. Indeed, as historian Janice Brown has stated, they were "unsung heroes," and perhaps the most important of them all was Ruth Corey. She was the daughter of Vermont natives Emma Ferris Corey and Charles Corey, a Manchester industrialist and owner of a needle factory.

As a young woman, Ruth Corey attended the Hillsborough County Nursing Program in Goffstown and graduated from there in 1917. In November of that year, she put her newly-learned skills to use for the greater good when she enlisted in the Army Nurse Corps. She was first sent to Camp Custer in Battle Creek, Michigan, to be trained in the ways of the military, as well as working at the base hospital there treating recently inducted soldiers. In September 1918, she was among a group of nurses sent to Europe, assigned to the newly-established Base Hospital #56 at Allerey in eastern France. This 1,800-bed hospital was both a surgical and treatment unit, specializing in dermatological cases and genitourinary diseases, but also treated Spanish flu patients and wounded from the Meuse-Argonne Offensive. Corey remained a nurse with this unit until it was disbanded in the spring of 1919, subsequently returning to the United States in April and given an honorable discharge from the Nurse Corps in June 1919.

Thereafter, she worked as a nurse for the Veteran's Bureau in Manchester and later, by 1930, was working as an X-ray nurse according to Federal Census records. While Ruth

Above left: Corey Family monument, Ruth Ferris Corey (1972), Pine Grove Cemetery, Manchester. (*Photo courtesy of John Wilby*)

Above right: Photograph of Ruth Ferris Corey, *c.* 1919, from *The Granite Monthly.*

Corey was now working as a civilian nurse, her army experience remained a part of her life. Not only did she treat veterans, but from the very end of her active military career also became deeply involved in establishing American Legion Post #2 in Manchester and was long an attendee at the New Hampshire veteran's reunions which were held annually at the Weirs. Of Ruth Corey, writer Paul Stacy commented that her "long and tireless service as a nurse entitles her to full membership in the Legion" and that a separate woman's post might have been established if the required fifteen members were not "engaged in work that takes them away from their homes." Nonetheless, Ruth Corey worked tirelessly as a veteran as well and was a trailblazer, becoming the first female American Legion delegate to a state convention in the organization's history.

Later in life, Ruth Corey, who never married, managed her family's estate. At her death, she was buried in the family plot in Pine Grove Cemetery, her name inscribed at the bottom of the family monument, her date of death left blank.

SHARON CHRISTA CORRIGAN MCAULIFFE (1948–1986), CALVARY CEMETERY, CONCORD

There is hardly a person of school-age or older in New Hampshire that has not heard of Christa McAuliffe, New Hampshire's Teacher in Space pioneer, but enough cannot be written about a woman who was destined for the stars, flying higher and further than any other New Hampshire woman had before.

She was born in Boston, the daughter of Grace George Corrigan and Edward Corrigan, her mother a teacher, her father an accountant. From her time as a young woman growing up in the Space Age 1960s, Christa was captivated by NASA's Mercury and Apollo projects. She attended Framingham State College in Massachusetts and gained her bachelor's degree in teaching in 1970, and after her marriage to high-school sweetheart Steven McAuliffe, the couple moved to Maryland. Here, Christa McAuliffe gained her master's degree from Bowie State College in 1978, continuing her career as an educator, teaching history and English.

The couple's first child, Scott, was born in 1976, and their daughter, Caroline, was born after their move to Concord, New Hampshire, in 1978. Working first at the junior high-school level before moving to Concord High School in 1983, McAuliffe was a popular history and English teacher who enriched her classes by bringing in outside speakers and organizing field trips. One of her key teaching points was the impact that ordinary citizens had on history, while she also taught a class whose curriculum was self-designed, emphasizing the achievement of women in American history. Not only was McAuliffe a gifted teacher, she was also a popular one, beloved by her students.

McAuliffe, too, had never lost her interest in space exploration, so when President Reagan announced the Teacher in Space program in 1984, Christa applied, filling out an eleven-page application, one of over 11,000 teachers to do so, stating in part: "I want to demystify NASA and spaceflight" and "I want students to see and understand the special perspective of space and relate it to them." McAuliffe's application was chosen as one of the 114 semi-finalists, two from each state and territory in the U.S., and her final selection for the Teacher in Space program was announced with much fanfare in July 1985 after having undergone medical examinations and being interviewed and evaluated by a NASA committee along with nine other finalists. By September, Christa McAuliffe was undergoing rigorous training at the Johnson Space Center in Houston, along with alternate Barbara Morgan, but also made public appearances from time to time on network morning news shows, as well as being interviewed by comedian Johnny Carson on *The Tonight Show*. She was an immediate hit with the media and the Teacher in Space Program gained a wide public audience as a result.

McAuliffe was assigned to the crew of the space shuttle *Challenger*, officially designated as a payload specialist. Her job would be, among others, to conduct several classes from space, which would be broadcast to millions of school-children, as well as offer a guided tour of the shuttle. The lesson plans that Christa would use were designed by herself, while she also intended to record a personal diary of her space experiences. Needless to say, the people of New Hampshire were extremely proud and supportive of McAuliffe, and the launching of the *Challenger* mission was eagerly awaited. Finally, the launch day came, January 28, 1986, when McAuliffe and six other shuttle crew boarded the space craft. Sadly, just seventy-three seconds after its launch, the space shuttle *Challenger* exploded, killing its entire crew instantly. The explosion of the *Challenger*, caused by a faulty component of the rocket booster, was not just a personal tragedy for the McAuliffe family; it was a national tragedy, hearkening back to the earlier losses in American space programs. However, the loss of McAuliffe and *Challenger* was in many ways an even greater blow to America, for millions of American school-children had watched the events of that tragic day unfold live on classroom TV. Indeed, many children who viewed McAuliffe's final moments to this day can still recall the event with an unusual clarity.

As a result of the *Challenger* disaster, the Teacher in Space Program was discontinued, and the entire Space Shuttle program was put on hold for a time. However, the impact of Christa McAuliffe on the national psyche was nonetheless profound; by her knowledge and enthusiasm for teaching, she inspired a whole generation of students to "reach for the stars" and there can be no doubt that she also inspired countless young girls to seek out careers in STEM fields. For her service, McAuliffe was posthumously awarded the Congressional Space Medal of Honor and in 2021 the Department of the Treasury issued a $1 silver commemorative coin in her honor. However, her biggest memorial, and lasting legacy, is the McAuliffe-Shepard Discovery Center in her hometown of Concord, which first opened in 1990 as the Christa McAuliffe Planetarium. Thousands of school children visit this living memorial annually to learn about space, just as McAuliffe would have wanted. Her gravesite in Cavalry Cemetery, consisting of a large block of polished black granite, is visited by countless numbers of people annually, many of them children who leave personal mementos in honor of their teacher-hero.

Elizabeth Ann Virgil (1903–1991), Harmony Grove Cemetery, Portsmouth

I first "met" Elizabeth Virgil while visiting Dimond Library on the campus of the University of New Hampshire at Durham many years ago. There, not far from the entrance, in a very public space, was (and still is) the stunning painting of Elizabeth Ann Virgil, whose appearance exudes to passers-by the qualities of determination, grace, and kindness. It was only later that I learned that she was the first person of color to graduate from a New Hampshire university.

Above: S. Christa McAuliffe, 1986, Cavalry Cemetery, Concord.

Right: Mission Specialist/Teacher in Space Christa McAuliffe, 1985. (*Courtesy of NASA*)

Elizabeth Ann Virgil was born in Plymouth, Massachusetts, the daughter of Alberta Curry Virgil (the daughter of slaves) and Wilcox Virgil, a native of the West Indies. Elizabeth's parents had met and married in Virginia, and while her father would return to Virginia, she and her older sister, Melvina, and their mother moved to Portsmouth in 1910. Alberta Virgil worked as a housekeeper and a cook for a local family to support her daughters. While her older sister would later become a cabaret dancer, Elizabeth had the desire to become a teacher. As she was growing up, it is said that her mother's employer, "a civic activist" in Portsmouth, "noticed her aptitude in school and desire to attend college," and subsequently helped her to gain a scholarship and the money required for books. She was admitted to the University of New Hampshire in 1922 and immediately became a stranger in an already strange land.

While there was a thriving African American community in Portsmouth, at the school she would attend in Durham, she was the only person of color. It must have been daunting, but Virgil was up for the challenge. Virgil's enrollment at UNH came at a time when the KKK was very active in New Hampshire, but she persevered and was a popular student. Though she could not join any sorority due to her race, her love of music compelled her to join several clubs, and she even formed her own singing group, the Treble Clefs. Elizabeth Virgil, too, was well-known for the high grades she achieved. In 1926, she made history by graduating with a degree in home economics.

Sadly, because of the racial prejudices and restrictions in New Hampshire at the time, Elizabeth could not teach school in the state and, so, she moved to moved to Virginia, where she gained employment in segregated school systems. She first taught at the Virginia Normal and Industrial Institute in Petersburg, and later in Bowie, Maryland, where she taught other young African Americans to become teachers in the rural south. Still later, she taught in North Carolina, and later returned northward, taking further classes in New York at the Columbia Teachers College. Though Virgil was employed in the south, she returned to her hometown in the summers to stay with her mother.

However, by 1940 Elizabeth Virgil was forced to return to New Hampshire permanently due to her mother's failing health and, despite her wealth of experience, she still could not teach in New Hampshire due to a color barrier, which would not be lifted until decades later. Instead, she supported her mother by first working a domestic, and later working at varied jobs in a doctor's office, as a demonstrator for gas appliances, and as a typist at the Portsmouth Naval Shipyard. In 1951, she began working for her *alma mater*, not as a teacher, but as a secretary in the Soil Conservation Department for UNH.

Never married, "Miss Virgil," as Elizabeth was affectionately known, was active in the Portsmouth community, playing the piano and organ at local events, singing in church choirs and choral groups, as well as remaining an active volunteer with the Red Cross, an activity she had begun many years previously in high school. One of the hallmarks of her life, as authors Valerie Cunningham and Mark Sammons note, was "to talk about goodness in people." Virgil retired from the University of New Hampshire in 1973, and in 1991, just the year before her death, was finally recognized by UNH for having broken one of New Hampshire's color barriers. To the very end, Elizabeth Ann Virgil was a strong believer in education and the goodness of people. She established at UNH the Alberta Curry Virgil scholarship in honor of her mother, and while she stated that "I set up the fund especially for my people," she also said "but its for anybody that wants it." And that picture of Elizabeth Ann Virgil, showing her with sheet music in hand and "her beloved piano" in the background? It was painted in her honor and placed in 1991, just months before her death.

Virgil Family monument, Elizabeth Ann Virgil (1991), Harmony Grove Cemetery, Portsmouth. Elizabeth's name is inscribed on the opposite side, with no death date listed.

Portrait painting of Elizabeth Ann Virgil by Grant Drumheller, 1991. (*Image courtesy of Milne Special Collections and Archives Department, University of New Hampshire Library, Durham*)

Source Bibliography

Part I

Bolles, S., *Early History of the Town of Bethlehem, New Hampshire* (Woodsville, NH: Enterprise Printing House, 1883)

Chase, T., and Gabel, L. K., *Gravestone Chronicles: Some eighteenth-century New England carvers and their work* (Boston: New England Historic Genealogical Society, 1997)

Knoblock, G. A., *Historic Burial Grounds of the New Hampshire Seacoast* (Charleston, SC: Arcadia Publishing, 1999)

Ludwig, A. I., *Graven Images: New England Stonecarving and its Symbols, 1650–1815* (Middletown, CT: Wesleyan University Press, 1966)

Main, G. L., "Naming Children in Early New England," *The Journal of Interdisciplinary History*, Vol. 27, No. 1 (Summer 1996), pp. 1-27

Noyes, S., Libby, C. T., and Davis, W. G., *Genealogical Dictionary of Maine and New Hampshire* (Boston: Genealogical Publishing Co., 1996)

Smith, A., *The Theory of Moral Sentiments* (Mineola, NY: Dover Publications, 2006 (1759))

Stearns, E., *History of the Town of Rindge, New Hampshire* (Boston: G.H. Ellis, 1875)

Tomsett, C. H., "A Note on the Economic Status of Widows in Colonial New York," *New York History*, Vol. 55, No. 3 (July 1974), pp. 319-332

Walvin, J., "Dust to Dust: Celebrations of Death in Victorian England," *Historical Reflections/ Reflections Historiques*, vol. 9, no. 3, 1982, pp. 353-371. JSTOR, www.jstor.org/stable/41298792

Part II

Annett, A., and Lehtinen, A. E., *History of Jaffrey (Middle Monadnock), New Hampshire* (Jaffrey, NH: Town of Jaffrey, 1937)

Bates College, *General Catalogue of Bates College and Cobb Divinity School 1863–1915* (Lewiston, ME: Bates College, 1915)

Biography.com, "Christa McAuliffe Biography," Biography.com, April 27, 2017, www.biography.com/astronaut/christa-mcauliffe

Brown, J. A., "Samuel Joy and His Spite Tombstone in Durham, New Hampshire," Cow Hampshire: New Hampshire's History Blog, April 16, 2018, www.cowhampshireblog.com/2018/04/16/

durham-new-hampshire-samuel-joy-and-his-spite-tombstone/; "New Hampshire WW I Nurse and First Delegate to American Legion Convention: Ruth Ferris Corey of Manchester," Cow Hampshire: New Hampshire's History Blog, July 24, 2018, www.cowhampshireblog. com/2018/07/24/new-hampshire-wwi-nurse-and-first-woman-delegate-to-american-legion-convention-ruth-ferris-corey-of-manchester/

Callahan, M., "Peyton Place's Real Victim," *Vanity Fair*, January 22, 2007, www.vanityfair.com/news/2006/03/peytonplace200603

Chang, R., "How Teacher Christa McAuliffe Was Chosen for the Disastrous Challenger Mission," Biography.com, September 15, 2020, www.biography.com/news/christa-mcauliffe-challenger-story

Chase, F., *A History of Dartmouth College and the Town of Hanover, New Hampshire* (Cambridge, MA: John Wilson and Son, University Press, 1891)

Child, H., (ed.), *Gazetteer of Grafton County, N.H., 1709–1886* (Syracuse, NY: Syracuse Journal, 1886)

Crawford, L., *The History of the White Mountains* (Portland, ME: B. Thurston, 1886 (1979))

Dearborn, J. J., *The History of Salisbury, New Hampshire* (Manchester, NH: William Moore, 1890)

Dedication of the Soldier's Monument at Peterboro, N.H. (Peterboro, NH: Farnum and Scott, 1870)

Duyckinck, E. A., and G. L., *Cyclopaedia of American Literature*, Vol. 1 (New York: Charles Scribner, 1856)

Gilbert, E., *History of Salem, N.H.* (Concord, NH: Rumford Press, 1907)

Goldfarb, B., *18 Tiny Deaths: The Untold Story of the Woman Who Invented Modern Forensics* (Naperville, IL: Sourcebooks, 2021)

Griffin, S. G., *A History of the Town of Keene from 1732* (Keene, NH: Sentinel Printing, 1904)

Hale, J. D., "So What's with this Molly Stark Woman Anyway?" *New England Today Living*, August 1, 2015, newengland.com/today/living/humor/so-whats-with-this-molly-stark-woman-anyway/

Haynes, M. A., *A History of the Second Regiment, New Hampshire Volunteer Infantry, in the War of the Rebellion* (Lakeport, NH: n.p., 1896)

History of Coos County, New Hampshire (Syracuse, NY: W.A. Fergusson, 1888)

Hutchinson, J. W., *Story of the Hutchinsons* (Boston: Lee and Shepard, 1896)

Jackman, L., *History of the Sixth New Hampshire Regiment in the War for the Union* (Concord, NH: Republican Press, 1891)

Johnson, P., McLean, R., and Streeter, M., *My Dearest Ira: Selections from the Letters and Diaries of Lucy and Ira Blake 1861–1864* (North Conway, NH: privately printed, 2014)

Johnson, S. W., *A Narrative of the Captivity of Mrs. Johnson* (Springfield, MA; H.R. Huntting Co, 1907 (1796))

Keeler, Rev. S. C., *The Murdered Maiden Student: A Tribute to the Memory of Miss Josie A. Langmaid* (Suncook, Pembroke, NH: Crum & Ringler, 1878)

Klepacki, L., *Avon: Building the World's Premier Company For Women* (Hoboken, NJ: John Wiley & Sons, 2005)

Knoblock, G. A., *African American Historic Burial Grounds and Gravesites of New England* (Jefferson, NC: McFarland & Co., 2016); *Portsmouth Cemeteries* (Charleston, SC: Arcadia Publishing, 2005)

Lord, C. C., *Life and Times in Hopkinton, N.H.* (Concord, NH: Republican Press, 1890)

Marvin, C., *Hanging Ruth Blay: An Eighteenth-Century New Hampshire Tragedy* (Charleston, SC: The History Press, 2010)

Merrill, G. D., (ed.), *History of Carroll County, New Hampshire* (Boston: W.A. Fergusson, 1907)

Morcom, R., "They All Loved Lucy," *American Heritage Magazine*, Vol. 21, Issue 6, October 1970

"New Hampshire Necrology: Augusta Harvey Worthen," *The Granite Monthly*, Vol. XLII, No. 7, July 1910, p. 223

Paradis, J., "You Asked, We Answered: What's the Story Behind That Mysterious Gravestone in New Boston," New Hampshire Public Radio, March 9, 2018, www.nhpr.org/post/you-asked-we-answered-whats-story-behind-mysterious-gravestone-new-boston#stream/0

Potter, C. E., *The History of Manchester, formerly Derryfield, in New Hampshire* (Manchester, NH: C.E. Potter, 1856)

Robinson, M. C., "Hannah Davis, a Pioneer Maker of Bandboxes," *Boston Evening Transcript*, Saturday, November 14, 1925

Rothman, D., "Savilla Jones and Henry Sargent-Love and Murder in New Boston," New Boston Historical Society, March 2018, www.newbostonhistoricalsociety.com/cemetery/Sevilla%20Jones%20and%20Henry%20Sargent.pdf

Sammons, M. J., and Cunningham, V., *Black Portsmouth: Three Centuries of African American Heritage* (Durham, NH: University of New Hampshire Press, 2004)

Schwartz, G., (ed.), *A Woman Doctor's Civil War: Esther Hill Hawk's Diary* (Columbia, SC: University of South Carolina Press, 1992)

Smith, A., *History of the Town of Peterborough* (Boston: George H. Ellis, 1876)

Smithsonian American Art Museum, "Murder is Her Hobby: Francis Lee Glessner and the Nutshell Studies of Unexplained Death," The Smithsonian Art Museum, americanart.si.edu/exhibitions/nutshells

Stacy, P. F., "The American Legion in New Hampshire," *The Granite Monthly*, vol. LI, December 1919, pp. 582-84

"Tabitha Tenney-New Hampshire's First Best-Selling Author," New England Historical Society, 2020, www.newenglandhistoricalsociety.com/tabitha-tenney-new-hampshire-first-best-selling-author/

"The Somnambulism Defense; The Sleepwalking Murderer of Pembroke," New England Historical Society, www.newenglandhistoricalsociety.com/somnambulism-defense-sleepwalking-murderer-pembroke/

Thompson, M. P., *Landmarks in Ancient Dover, New Hampshire* (Durham, NH: Republican Press, 1892)

Waite, F. C., "Dr. Lucinda Sussannah (Capen) Hall," *New England Journal of Medicine*, March 22, 1934, pp. 644-47

Wheeler, E., *The History of Newport, New Hampshire* (Concord, NH: Republican Press, 1879)

Willard, F., and Livermore, M., *A Woman of the Century: Fourteen Hundred-Seventy Biographical Sketches of Leading American Women* (Buffalo, NY: Charles Wells Moulton, 1893)

Woodward, M., "First in Courage; Elizabeth Virgil '26 quietly brough integration to UNH," *UNH Magazine* Online, Spring 2007, unhmagazine.unh.edu/sp07/historypage.html

Worthen, A. H., *The History of Sutton, New Hampshire* (Concord, NH: Republican Press, 1890)